Personal Wisdom

Also by Robert Brown

Updated Edition

Personal Wisdom

Making Sense of You
Others and the
Meaning of Life

Robert Brown

Denro Classics

While the author and publisher made their best effort to accuracy and completeness, they make no representation or warranty of the material for any particular purpose. The advice, tools and strategies contained herein may not be suitable for your situation. You should consult the appropriate professional when needed. The author has taken reasonable precautions in the preparation of this book and believes the facts presented within to be accurate, however, neither the author nor the publisher assumes any responsibility for errors or omissions. The author and publisher specifically disclaim any liability resulting from the use or application of the information contained in this book.

Requests for permission to use or reproduce material from this book should be addressed to collectivewisdom2020@gmail.com

Published by Denro Classics
1700 Mukilteo Speedway #201, 1084
Mukilteo WA 98275
USA

Library of Congress Control Number: 2019932520

ISBN-13 978-0-9998667-4-0

To Barbara Asperger and the memory of Bill Brown,
my older sister and younger brother

One's first step in wisdom is to question everything—and one's last step is to come to terms with everything.

Gerog Christoph Lichtenberg

The Beginning

When I was 17, while a senior in high school sitting in social studies class watching a scratchy black and white documentary film of WW II, I suffered a trauma. No one else in class did, just me. The film showed the usual bombs dropping out of airplanes, big guns firing shells, and buildings collapsing into piles of bricks and billowing smoke. Then the scene changed.

It switched to show an industrial site and a man kneeling on stones between two sets of railroad tracks. He was an American pilot, captured by the Japanese. A soldier walks in from the right carrying a rifle, gets close and points it at the knelling man, and shoots him in the back of the head. The pilot fell to the side and lay there, the soldier walked away as casually as if he had just bought a loaf of bread. I was stunned.

Everyone else wondered if the movie material would be on the test. I began wondering about the fragility of life and what people are capable of doing to one another. Questions arose: Is life worth living? Is there a best life? Who has the answers? Those kinds of questions began my life-long quest to understand life and what to do about it. A lot of time has passed since then, more behind me than ahead. I'm pleased to share what I know and have learned. You will hear from ancient philosophers, modern scientists, psychologists, writers, many others, and me.

At this moment, I am seventy-three-years-old and have been seventy-three for six months. My hair is mostly silver and thinning on top. My skin seems to become more mottled every day. The print in newspapers keeps getting smaller and a five-pound sack of potatoes is heavier than it used to be.

It's almost embarrassing to be sneaking into the mid-seventies and not be anything like I pictured this age to be. I don't look like Cary Grant. I don't have the mystic wisdom of a leather-skinned Apache chief. And I don't own an estate by the seashore where all the family can gather for long weekends. In fact, I'm in that challenging transition where my kids are telling me what computer to buy and coming over to the house to fix things I don't seem able to figure out. But, their worries to the contrary, I do have my lucid moments.

Right now, I'm thinking of you. I'm wondering what you're hoping to get out of this book, how your life may change by what you learn. I will give you ideas and tools of proven value for the whole of your life, ones that have worked for me and many others over almost 60 years.

Self-help books usually identify a problem, such as destructive relationships, low self-esteem or anxiety, and provide solutions, often with a to-do list of specific actions.

Personal Wisdom is a self-help book, but with a significant difference. This one presents an opportunity; how to live a life unique to you.

You have a burden unique to humans. The burden is *you must decide what is important.* How well you choose determines the value of your life. This book will not focus on a single problem. It will give you the understanding and the tools to create a life unique to you. What will make your life truly yours? There are three tasks you must undertake: become independent, clarify your perspective and develop effective life skills.

INDEPENDENCE

You must become independent, unencumbered by the expectations of others. To be you and no one else, you must gain personal wisdom; your wisdom, not everyone else's all mashed together. In the first sections of the book, you will learn to free yourself from old ideas that are not yours but determined who you have become anyway. Your cultural roots defined you even before you existed. It's as if you were born into a play already begun, with your role already determined and your world a stage already set. The *You* section will help you design your own stage and create the right role for you.

PERSPECTIVE

You must continually enrich your perspective, notice changes, respond to them, and improve yourself. In a world connected to others as much as ours, you must be able to identify and resist the forces (what we'll call the "wind") that push and pull you every day. The *Others* section will help you figure out what is important in the moment and in the long run and create a new personal perspective. The clearer your perspective, the better you can understand what you see and the better you can choose and do what is important.

SKILLS

Last, you must become as effective as possible. You must be able to do the important things well. You can live your ideal life by knowing what is right and by using your life skills. The two *Skills* sections teach you how to be your best self, interact well with others and create meaning when you get out of bed in the morning. You can live a more fulfilling life, achieve more success at work, create more harmony at home, and connect more closely to those you love.

PERSONAL WISDOM

Personal Wisdom will help you find true knowledge about yourself and what is important for your life. You will live your life from this new knowledge, rather than the haphazard accumulation of opinions, guesses and assumptions that have guided your existence until now.

Since your life is important and we both want you to make the best of it, we need to take a clear-eyed look at you; the kind of examination a physician would perform with bright lights and cold metal instruments. In a way, we're looking for malignancies, the kinds of things that rob you of precious days and even years.

Gaining personal wisdom should be pleasant. But it will require work, or more accurately, effort, on your part. This is not a book to rest on your bedside nightstand to peruse a few pages before dozing off. If you are serious about living your ideal life, then a good way is to follow the format set out for you. Do not simply read the book or think about the activities. Do what it suggests. If you do, you will begin the rewarding and lifelong quest to live a life perfect for you.

HOPE

One of my professors in psychology graduate school, Viennese Psychiatrist Viktor Frankl, talked about hope in his book, *Man's Search for Meaning.* He described his and others' lives in a Nazi concentration camp and the importance of hope in such a place of despair. He said in this book, "Everything can be taken from a man but... the last of the human freedoms—to choose one's attitude in any set of circumstances, to choose one's own way." That is what this book is about, too.

If you're dealing with significant problems, no matter what they are, *Personal Wisdom* can help you have hope that you will succeed. Although not designed for specific problems, this approach will strengthen you for all life's eventualities. It's like eating right and exercising is good for you no matter what. Developing personal wisdom is helpful in your life, no matter what.

A hopeful life is not one that avoids pain, minimizes errors or acquires wealth. A hopeful life is when you are knocked down a hundred times and get back on your feet a hundred and one times. Hope is what brings you back.

Hope tells you you're not bad just because you make mistakes. Hope enables you to make the right choices after making many bad ones. Hope enables you to learn, and teach.

Second only to love, hope makes life worth living.

As you read the material you will develop greater personal wisdom, create better memories, adjust more easily to your fortunes, be a better friend, sleep better at night, be more alive during the day, and live the best life for you.

Discuss what you have read with others. The more you

do beyond reading, the better your life can become. Skip sections if you wish. You're the boss, but do as well as you can, make each decision one you'll be pleased with.

WHY THIS BOOK

People like you have been asking important questions about life, what it is, what it means, how to live it, for thousands of years. You would think we would have the answers by now. We do and they are much more personalized than you might think.

Brilliant people have proposed ideas. Equally brilliant people have proposed opposing ideas. Life is not one size fits all. What life is the right fit for you? Only you can answer:

- Who am I?
- Where am I going?
- How will I get there?

According to recent estimates, there have been 108.2 billion human beings, making you one tiny drop in a very large ocean. Too many of those billions lived their lives as tiny drops in a big sea, floating along with everyone else. Be different. If you want a life full of meaning, happiness, intimacy, fulfillment, compassion, joy and doing things of lasting value, you have come to the right place.

There is a secret to living your ideal life, easy to explain; the challenge is discovering how to do it your way. Here it is:

Awareness + Skills $\longrightarrow$ Your Ideal Life

Awareness is of who you want to be and the positive and negative power of people around you. The skills are to express yourself well and interact effectively with others. No one can teach you how to live your best, that must come from your experience, but this book, in as practical a way as possible, will help you make better sense of you and your world.

We'll begin with one of those brilliant people who proposed good answers quite a while ago.

Before you were born, just as America was being born, in the late 1500s, in a tiny room high in a French castle, Michel Eyquem de Montaigne, Lord of Montaigne, was wondering the same things you are.

Few know of him these days, but many people you may have heard of were influenced by his thoughts. They include Francis Bacon, René Descartes, Blaise Pascal, Jean-Jacques Rousseau, Ralph Waldo Emerson, Friedrich Nietzsche, Isaac Asimov, maybe William Shakespeare, me, and now you.

Montaigne sought for years to understand life and concluded he could understand only his own, and not much of that. The same is true for you. Perhaps his most famous quote is, "What do I know?" He meant that you and everyone else will never know all you wish to know yet can live a wonderful life, anyway. He also said:

There is no knowledge so hard to acquire as the knowledge of how to live this life well and naturally.

Here are his thoughts translated for the 21st century and our effort to understand you, others and the meaning of life.

1. Personal wisdom is gaining the knowledge to live your unique life.
2. Your unique life will always be evolving.
3. You can never be sure you're living your ideal life.
4. No one else knows what's best for you.

5. Just about everyone is ready with an opinion.

Personal Wisdom will help you discover the secret to your life. Only your life, no one else's. This is your opportunity to learn life skills, use them, and enjoy a meaningful life; one created for you, by you.

Contents

OTHERS

Other people do not want you to be independent, they want you to be like them and you fall for their tricks. In this section you will learn about the powerful forces around you and how to overcome them.

LIFE SKILLS II

Meaningfully connecting with others adds the critical touch to the joy of life.

> This is a more personal and detailed look at *You* and *Others*, so you have an additional way of becoming independent and redesigning who you are, where you are going and how to get there.

LIFE

LIFE

An unexamined life is not worth living.
Plato

Life is a mystery. None of us did anything to make it happen. Without warning, we slip into life one day, make our way through it, and eventually stop living, sometimes while we're still alive.

We are made of cosmic dust from a biochemical recipe handed down from millions of years ago. And although the ingredients are the same, the recipe has infinite variations.

Each of us is unique, yet similar to all. We see the same night sky as our grandparents and dream the same dreams as the pharaohs. Parts of me are identical to parts of you. We feel the same pain, the same joys, and ask the same questions.

But we don't follow the same paths. You know things I don't. You grasp ideas I wouldn't understand. You have done things that would amaze me, and I may have amazed you too.

We come in different sizes, shapes, IQs, races, attitudes, nationalities, temperaments, and just about everything else. What we all have in common is this experience we call life. Some see it as a burden, others a gift. What your life is, depends on you.

If for no other reason, your life is precious because it will end. Before it ends, whether this is a long time or all too brief, you decide how to define your life and what should be done with it.

Life isn't what you experience but the decisions you make.

By what you chose, you add something to your identity and character like so many coats of paint or, more gracefully, like layers on a pearl. You change every day, maybe improving, maybe becoming worse, or maybe becoming stagnant. Your life is made up of thousands of moments where you chose one way over another. The effect of these decisions can last a few minutes when choosing corn flakes for breakfast or for a lifetime when proposing marriage to the love of your life. Until you die and there are no more decisions, your choices mean everything.

Death is the reason I wrote this book. I was haunted by the images of the executed pilot mentioned earlier, the pointed rifle, the man lying dead, the casual turning away.

These images made me realize that life can be horrific, and life ends, often without warning and often without dignity or meaning. Because we die, what we do while alive gains profound importance. We must do it right, in a limited time and often with limited resources. Death ends all possibilities. While you are alive, you must create personal meaning, or you have wasted the reason for your existence.

A friend of mine died a while ago. Before heading out for an hour's bike ride one Sunday morning, he kissed his wife in the kitchen who was stirring up pancakes for their two kids. That was the last kiss he would give her. While coasting down a hill on his way home, his wheels slipped on loose sand that had blown over the road. He fell and hit his head on the pavement. Rushed to the hospital, he was given aid in the emergency room and moved into intensive care. It soon became clear his brain no longer functioned. His wife allowed the many tubes and wires to be disconnected and he died.

At his funeral, one of his friends stood at the lectern and compared life to a novel. "No one," he said, "asks how long a book is. We want to know how good, how interesting, how worthwhile it is." He said our friend may have had a short life, but it was of value because of his contributions to the community and his many loving relationships.

We all have an idea of what the end will be like. No longer do our bodies wear out and die of old age. We will succumb to some well-defined clinical process. Heart disease will be the end for many of us, with cancer the next greatest killer and stroke third.

Often, the ending of life is a slow process of hardening arteries, deteriorating organs and thinning bones. There may be pain that makes us gasp with every step. We might forget the name of a friend and then who she is. These and many other elements of disease narrow the boundaries of our world and chip away at our quality of life. The end probably will not be pleasant or dignified.

I used to think having a dignified death was important; the kind where the family gathers around the deathbed to hear your last words of wisdom and to express their love before the final goodbyes. I worried that a bad death, like lying unresponsive for months in intensive care or slipping in the shower, banging my head, and lying there naked would diminish an otherwise satisfactory life.

I came to realize both the beginning and end of life are

relatively unimportant. The portion of life we have the most control over is the middle part, where we have the time and the opportunity to figure out who we are and what we want to do.

Our job, it seems to me, is to do this middle part well, adding value to our existence as we collect our personal moments. Wouldn't it be nice to live a life you know you can be proud of, now and later? This idea raises some interesting questions.

- Do you think your life should have meaning?
- Do you think others' lives have meaning?
- What makes your life important?
- Is your value found in your pants size, your income, likes on Facebook, how clean your house is or how smooth your skin feels?
- How much time should you spend working compared to eating, sleeping, relaxing, drinking a nice wine and making love?
- What would you do today if you knew you would die tomorrow?

In high school, I began seeking answers to such questions. Studying philosophy led to college courses in psychology, the science of human behavior and being awarded a Ph.D. in 1973. I searched for answers to the question I phrased in my mind as "why should people get out of bed in the morning?"

I sought the one, universal and eternal answer. I tried out concepts like value, truth, contentment, meaning, serving God, serving humankind, avoiding trouble, and minimizing pain. I also learned about people trying to survive another day, raise children, find food, and stay warm and dry.

Personal Wisdom is asking the questions, knowing the answers, testing those answers every day, and having the courage to change the answers and even the questions when they are no longer the right ones.

Choosing You

If not you, who?
If not now, when?
Hillel the Elder

It was still dark when the digital clock flipped to 4:30 and began its irritating buzz. Rachael opened her eyes. Her husband's plane would land at 10. There wasn't time to waste.

She rolled out of bed, tossed off her pajamas, jumped into the shower, spending an extra moment conditioning her hair. She put on a dress he liked (two weeks was a long business trip) and added a quick mist of his favorite scent. When she looked in the mirror, she had to admit, she looked good.

The drive to the airport was a pleasure. Classic rock was on the radio. Traffic was light. She cruised just above the speed limit. Along the way, she noticed how the sun sparkled off her engagement and wedding rings. She was so happy to be married to this man. Rachael sighed. The only thing missing was a child, maybe two or three. But it was too early. They both wanted children. That would happen.

Normal stuff for a woman married only five months, right? Seems like it but look again at her activities. How much of Rachael's actions were because of a conscious choice and how much was her behavior controlled by her culture? What did Rachael do as a unique, independent human and what did she do because it never occurred to her to consider anything else? Think for a moment about these elements:

Getting up to a digital clock
Staying at home while her husband traveled
Wearing pajamas
Taking a morning shower
Hair conditioner
Perfume
Using a mirror
Wearing a dress
Wearing a dress for her husband
Classic rock music
Speed limits
Driving just above the speed limit
Engagement and wedding rings
Marriage
Wanting children
Wanting two or three children
Wanting children later

What forces have been molding Rachael from the time she was born? How independent is she? Would Rachael be upset if she couldn't take her morning shower? How come? Would missing a shower make her reunion with her husband less pleasant?

Rachael is a twenty-six-year-old homemaker from Cleveland, Ohio. What if she lived in a yurt on the high plains of Mongolia? Would her behavior and expectations be different? Yes, they would, a lot. That's because cultural expectations would be different. The same is true if she were richer, poorer, older, younger, even if she was a different color.

You are much more controlled than you realize by unseen strings pulled by people you know and maybe worse, controlled by unseen strings pulled by people you don't know and who never knew you.

The world and all its components, nationalism, cultural norms, religious expectations, gender roles, and many, many others exist for you to follow, or not. Do some of your personal values conflict with your cultural values? Is it a case of black and white, right or wrong, and you or them, or is it your way *and maybe* their way?

There are advantages in believing whole-heartedly in your religion, your country, your political party or your ethnic group. Unquestioned faith in anything leads to security, optimism and a comforting sense of belonging. The individual becomes a cog in an important wheel. We all accept some portion of these forces.

The question is what percentage of your heritage is right for you and what percentage should you consider giving up to become independent.

Independence is about gaining wisdom about you, what's inside, what your boundaries are and where everyone else's boundaries end. Independence is knowing what is true and what is done because it was always done that way.

Here's a story from England from the 1960s, but it applies to all of us now.

A new employee had the job of filling out

various data forms. One form had been copied so often he couldn't make out the instructions for a box on the upper right. He went to a long-time employee for advice. "Oh, just put zero in it." So, he did, and all was fine. Each month he put a zero in the box and each month his report was accepted. Curiosity, however, wouldn't let up. He had to find out what the box was for. He searched the archives for clearer copies and found a twenty-year-old original that had directions for filling in the box. "Number of air-raids," it wanted to know.

Every day we do things that make little sense, but we do them without question. An independent life is free of unknown influences. That's simple enough to understand. The hard part is identifying the unknown influences so you can make informed choices about them. That's what we'll do next.

Q and A

Bob, I'm reading this book because I want to live my ideal life and I'm curious about your ideas. Are yours different from what I've already heard?

Good question. I learned some ideas in the book in graduate school. I thought they were profound, and they have resonated with me for the past forty years. Other ideas are from my mentors, many from clients and some I created. The bottom line is, you can learn from everyone, but along the way, you need to decide what's best for you.

Aren't there a million books already on the subject?

Yes, the difficulty is for the readers, the seekers, to find those that speak to them. There are many sources of wisdom, this is only one. Keep in mind we're looking at the big picture, your life as a whole. Not many do that.

I've done well with my life to date. Do you expect me to change who I am and what I do?

Absolutely. If you're not changing as you learn and grow, you're not doing it right. The trick is to know what to keep and what to change.

My values, like religion, are strong. Do you want me to examine my faith too?

Yes, I do. I don't think religion should entail blind faith; accepting everything without study or regard to consequences. Too often, malevolent human forces jumble God's words.

What's most important?

I have a lot of ideas on that. Let's keep looking at becoming independent. You must figure out where you fit and don't fit in the life designed for you by people who never knew you. You should decide, not them.

YOU

Roots

*Do not seek to follow in the
footsteps of the men of old;
Seek what they sought.*
Matsuo Basho

I can't do that!"

"Why not?"

"I don't know. I just can't."

Good grief, I thought, my last client after a long day and he acts as if I'm asking him to repaint the Sistine Chapel. I wanted him to talk to his wife. That seemed simple enough. "Look, George, all I'm suggesting is that you tell her how you feel."

"I can't. If I tell her I don't like it, it will hurt her feelings. She'll feel terrible and I'll feel like the bad guy."

George's reluctance to express his feelings to his wife of ten years was first created in the fourth grade while watching the Lone Ranger rescue another damsel-in-distress on TV. The Lone Ranger never did wrong, never got angry, and never hurt the girl. George wanted to run his life the way the Lone Ranger did. He didn't know that, and neither did I at the time.

Just as the laws of physics govern airplanes, popcorn and all the planets, dozens and dozens of societal expectations (call them rules) control you. These expectations show you how to fit in, how to succeed, how to relate to others and otherwise live a productive life.

However, other societal expectations are mean-spirited and destructive. Your roots are made up of hundreds, maybe thousands of rules, those that have stood the test of time and are invaluable, and others that appear good, but are harmful to you, and could be bad for everyone.

Do you want your life run by majority vote of a few million ancestors and their neighbors, none of whom you ever heard of and none who ever heard of you? That's what your roots are. Worse, all those people making the rules are dead, having lived in a time much different from yours, but who have a full vote anyway, every day of your life.

To live your ideal life, you must identify these rules, and like a flat tire, the inadequate ones must be changed for new rules that work better. When these rules are identified, they can be more easily understood and followed, or altered if they no longer serve any useful purpose.

Roots exist for all of us, but we each have our own version. Overcoming our roots is a lot like learning to ride a bicycle. Once you get the hang of it, it's easy, but, oh boy, those first few wobbly ventures around the block!

Every day, friends fight and make up, ordinary people perform heroic acts, a crowd becomes a mob, strangers fall in love, lovers hurt one another, parents teach their children, the world wakes up for another go-round. No one is born with the secret of what life is all about and how to do it right. No one is always there to help you make the best decision. But there is a script for you to follow and shoes to fill that are not your size.

Your roots cling hard to the past. They are a great ponderous weight determining what you are allowed to see, where you are allowed to go, and what you are allowed to do.

Your roots are a network, an interlocking morass of expectations and convention, controlling everyone to varying degrees. All of us want to live well, be happy, have friends, and enjoy success. Most of us would acknowledge that we do okay and know of others who have not been so lucky. And I think we would all admit that we could do better with a little more effort.

What is the difference between success and failure, between fulfillment and despair, between living your ideal life and everything else? Let me tell you about the first time I saw Alice.

ALICE

My consulting room was comfortable, a place to find trust and caring and to discover answers. It was like a living room with a couch, love seat, matching chairs, end tables, and lots of plants. I wanted people to be at peace there.

Alice couldn't find any. She wanted to die. Sitting on the edge of the couch, dressed in a plain skirt and simple blouse, she was my first client on a warm, blue-sky, Southern California day.

To look at her, one would assume this woman loved life and enjoyed it to the fullest. She shook my hand strongly, thanked me for seeing her on short notice, and sat down, then looked at me with sudden tears in her eyes.

"I don't know what to do," she cried and began to sob.

Her hands covered her face. "There's no place I can go. There is nothing I can do. I'm so miserable." She looked up at me, praying I could help.

That morning Alice told me that every effort toward well-being left the bitter taste of failure. Any success was an accident, something to distrust. Twenty compliments were washed away by an offhand criticism. Each morning she awoke to the promise of more despair.

Alice believed her life had become a series of punishments. Suicide, just to stop the pain, became a frightening option, a daily thought.

"But I don't want to die," she said. "I know that my life should be good," she added as she composed herself. "I'm not any worse off than anyone else. In fact, I'm better off than most people."

She continued to tell me how unhappy she was, and how that made little sense since there was no difference between her and her friends. Over her next few visits, we began to figure things out.

"It seems like my friends can handle things so much better than I can," she said. "Problems they cope with seem to get me down."

"Why is that?" I asked.

"I just see things differently, I guess."

"What do you mean?"

"Well, if my friend Jan has a problem, she just shrugs and says that tomorrow will be a better day. I can't do that. I have to figure out what to do about the problem now."

"How come?"

"It's like... well... My father used to have a saying, 'A place for everything and everything in its place.' So, I can't just let things sit. I feel like things have to be done now, right away, or I get upset."

"So, if you have a problem, you need to figure out what

to do about it right away?"

"Yeah. I know it sounds silly. I realize that you can't always do that, especially with major decisions, but that's what I expect of myself."

"Your mind would say, 'I should wait until next week to decide' and your emotions say, 'figure it out now or you're no good.'"

"Exactly," Alice replied.

"So, you feel you have to do things, resolve things, immediately, even when you know you can't."

"Well... yes. That doesn't sound like a good idea, does it?"

Alice and I began to explore what things she "has to do" and learned about the pressure she put on herself that her friends like Jan would never feel. We learned her rules of conduct were rigid, strict, punitive, and allowed little chance of success.

She expected herself to know all the answers, to make all things better, to always have the solution, and always do the right thing, and always do it right now.

"Nobody's perfect," she would say, all the while expecting herself to be without fault.

Once she realized her rules and guidelines were self-defeating, Alice began to redefine how to judge her efforts. She began to understand how her expectations were impossible to fulfill and thus, why she always fell short. Alice's rule changed from "do it now" to "do as well as I can."

Before she changed, Alice did what we all do, follow the rules we learned as children. But she followed them to almost tragic consequences. By the time she sought help her self-esteem was near zero.

How can someone get so far off track?

The answer lies in our basic set of life assumptions, the deep-seated mass of our roots that may no longer be right for us. If fact, logically, they cannot all be right for us. Some will have to go.

Rules

Life isn't about finding yourself. Life is about creating yourself.
George Bernard Shaw.

When we are children, we are rule-followers. Parents, teachers, adults and older children have all the power and control. We trust that these more mature people know how the world works and what is best for us. Others tell us when to get up and what to eat. Our efforts at school and a hundred other activities are monitored and evaluated. We learn to respond to encouraging words, gold stars and timeouts.

As we get older, we figure out beforehand what will probably work and what will get us into trouble. We learn to eat only so much candy, not talk back to the teacher, not leave tools out in the rain, get home by curfew, do homework ahead of time. Sometimes we're wrong. A few teenagers think you can't get pregnant the first time you do it or if you do it standing up. Sometimes as kids we make up our own answers of what to do and not do until we find ourselves bruised and bleeding at the bottom of a hill with a broken bike or being yelled at by an angry neighbor for a broken window.

During the "terrible twos," we realize we can impact our surroundings. We're told, "Don't push that button," we look up, smile, and push it. Through the turmoil of adolescence, we learn to be independent. We shift from being dependent rule-followers to independent rule-makers. When done well, this process establishes effective rules and abandons to immaturity the bad ones.

Alice didn't become an adult rule-maker. She tried to stretch a simple and sensible rule taught to her by a loving father, "a place for everything and everything in its place," way beyond its useful limits. What was right for a little girl's toys was inadequate for how an adult must decide about buying a house.

Some people avoid Alice's dilemma by learning effective rules that nurture and support and act as guides for living. These folks learn rules that are strong enough to weather a lifetime of trouble and turmoil. Living by the Golden Rule is a good example.

On the other hand, some people are compelled to conduct a lifelong jitterbug of wearing the latest fashions, rebelling against tradition, or ordering the hottest new drink in a trendy restaurant. They are obeying the rule "if you're not hip, you're nothing." Individuals who live their lives according to this rule are fearfully inadequate on their own and require constant reassurance from friends and admirers.

Any set of rules that depends on the authority of others will cause difficulties. The Marines, for example, "build men," many who later find civilian life decadent and unacceptable, sometimes unnerving. Strong identification with a group can also lead to sudden mob behavior, as sometimes happens at sporting events. Or group thinking can proceed at a slower pace, but with deadly results. The Jones cult mass suicide in South America is a sad example, as were the Heaven's Gate deaths in Rancho Santa Fe, California.

As long as the person doesn't encounter more than her rules can handle, she will never realize how limiting or destructive they could be. And though many childhood rules work well enough to be part of our adult value system, many of them can be limiting.

Several women I know did not go to college or get advanced training because they lived by the rule that girls should grow up to get married and have children. Some of them met and married men who lived by the rule that men work to support the family and the wife stays home to raise it. These folks stayed happy if both sets of rules remained the same. They became unhappily married or divorced if one or the other's rules changed.

Now, more than ever, one of life's most difficult problems is figuring out what rules should change with the times and which tried-and-true values should never be compromised. Abortion, assisted suicide, stem cell research, organ harvesting, designer babies and many other social, ethical and moral issues will continue to arise as technology outpaces the rules of our society.

We must be able to modernize old rules as we develop, individually and as a society, and keep the ones that have enduring value.

Do you know if your rules are those of a child rule-follower or an adult rule-maker? Can you tell one from the other?

ASSUMPTIONS

To illustrate our concept and have a little fun, try the riddle below. You must figure out how the fellow could leave the bar satisfied. Notice how your assumptions lead you astray.

> A man walks into a bar and asks the bartender for a glass of water. The bartender pulls out a pistol and points it at the man. The fellow thanks the bartender and leaves the bar satisfied. How can this be?

Most people guess that the bartender pulled out a water pistol, combining the water and the gun. But that isn't right. Like all riddles, to find the answer, you must evaluate your assumptions to avoid false ones that mislead. For example, most people assume that the fellow asking for the glass of water must be thirsty. Right? Nope. "Oh, okay," you think. If he isn't thirsty, he will not drink the water. If he isn't going to drink it, he must want it for something else. Maybe he wants the water to put out a fire or clean up a spill. Logical assumptions, but wrong. He isn't thirsty, but he wants to drink the water. I'll tell you more about the riddle later.

Do you see how assumptions can lead you down blind alleys? Unless you are aware of your assumptions, you won't figure out the riddle. You will go off in wrong directions, get frustrated, and want to give up. Life is the same way.

Unless you are aware of your assumptions about yourself and the world around you, your life path can be a series of blind alleys or blind luck. Not a good way of running a life.

We assume a lot of things: that the sun will come up tomorrow, that our shoe size today is the same as it was yesterday, and that life will have its difficulties. Assumptions help us define and predict what will happen this afternoon and next week. But you should be able to rely on truthful and valid assumptions, not the collection of truths, half-truths and outright lies that make up your roots.

For example, assuming most people will follow the rules allows you to trust that the other driver approaching a red signal light will stop and permit you to continue through the intersection on the green light. That assumption, although usually true, creates serious consequences when it proves to be false and that other person runs the red light.

Assumptions about ourselves can be self-limiting. The assumption "I could never get into medical school" has kept many potential excellent physicians working below their abilities, limiting them and their contributions to us all. Likewise, our assumptions about others have restricted their freedom to develop; minority races and women can attest to this consequence of bias and prejudice on the societal level, while you have probably endured forms of prejudice as an individual.

WHERE YOUR ROOTS CAME FROM

A good way of conceptualizing your roots is to define them as society's collection of "rules," powerful principles that define how we see ourselves and the dimensions of our world. Your roots tell you what you can and cannot do, what is important and what is not allowed. Roots are the foundation for our security as children and our roadmap into adulthood. They can become a prison. We can stand only in place, unable to leap and dance. I see them too as a great weight of expectations on our shoulders and a heavy pull on our hearts from guilt and shame and remorse. I also see them as a great heavy book of rules five feet tall, three feet wide and a thousand pages thick, bound in leather and edged in gold, written by everyone that came before.

Some classic sources of our roots to make sense of the world include the 3,000-year-old *I Ching*, the *Upanishads*, *Ecclesiastes*, and the *Proverbs of Solomon*.

We absorb rules from what our parents do, we learn them from books, we accept them from what our teachers tell us, and we create them from our best guess of what makes sense. Our rules should evolve as we grow up, not force us to act like everyone else. These rules are all in our head, so ingrained that we don't realize they were made up; some a long time ago; five hundred, a thousand years ago and more.

You will live your ideal life only if you identify, understand, and then control your personal rules. Most people don't, thus weighing down their dreams with leg irons of incorrect and outdated ideas. Roots are automatic and invisible. They seem like reality only because we don't know better. It's very much like when I was an 11th grader and my sister got glasses. I tried them on and looked across the street. I could see the numbers on the houses! Only at that moment did my parents and I realize how poor my eyesight was. Roots are like that. You don't notice what you can't see.

You may know people who are wasting their talents and living below their potential, like Tom.

Tom is an acoustic guitarist and a baritone who melts female hearts. He loves playing and singing for friends and occasionally at clubs but has never pursued a professional career. He never felt good enough. Since he very much wanted a musical career, he has been waiting for someone to discover him.

One clump of his roots was that if he had to push for recognition, he wasn't talented, he was just pushy. Only if an expert managed to find him and guide his career would he be truly good. He's still waiting to be discovered. Tom and others like him are following personal rules established as children. They follow these rules without ever thinking they have other choices. You do this to a degree. We all do. It's time to pull out the gardening shears.

Pruning your Roots

L ook how a simple assumption can fool science. There is a classic experiment in psychology that compares smart and dumb rats. The scientist creates two groups of lab rats, A and B, of ten each. He labels Group A as the smart group and B as the dumb group or vice versa; it doesn't matter. Then he goes to a graduate student he wants to fool and says, "Group A has been bred for intelligence and Group B has not. I want you to find out how much smarter the smart rats are in learning a maze." And, as we've learned from research, the smart group seems to learn the maze faster. This happens because the graduate student expects it to happen.

Because the student assumed one group was smarter than the other, that's what happened. A stopwatch is pressed a little quicker in the laboratory for the smart rats, or, in the real world, pretty Naomi is encouraged a little more than ugly Anna in the classroom. This happens with smart rats, attractive kids, tall employees, and people who are different. Whatever the differences, we tend to make one a winner and the other a loser. This kind of thing may have happened to you.

The term for this is, "self-fulfilling prophecy": What you think should happen you make happen. That is how Ouija boards work and how too many human lives are run. Eric Berne, the founder of Transactional Analysis, popularized this idea as personal scripts. Over time, from personal experiences and cultural expectations, a person formulates how his life should be, what Berne called his script, and goes about making sure he plays the part. This script has nothing to do with reality or even fate, it is what we subconsciously decided should happen and we behave and interpret life in a way that makes this script come true.

Many people have a script like, "I will be like my father" or "Life will hold no happiness for me." As you may guess, these scripts can be powerful and destructive. They always limit a person's potential and freedom to change. Your rules form the basis of what you can do with your existence. Your script is how you live your rules. Someone who operates from the assumption that "life holds no happiness" will make decisions that prove the truth of that assumption. We see what we expect to see, make happen what we think should happen, and do what "feels right." That's how human nature works and how your rules work.

A woman breaks away from the grasp of two strong men to run into a burning building. Rule: "My children are more important than my life." Four honor-roll teenage boys rob a small grocery store. Rule: "A real man doesn't back down from a dare." On a smaller scale, a twelve-year-old fights her parents tooth and nail, making everyone miserable for days, to convince them to buy her a yellow sweater. Her rule was "I've got to be like everyone else or I'm a nobody."

BURIED RULES

The above were examples of some obvious and simple rules. Each of us has dozens of subtler and more influential rules buried in our subconscious. A woman client and I worked together for weeks before we learned why she continued to stay with a man who abused her. We figured out that one of her buried rules was "If your marriage doesn't work, you're a failure as a woman." A second rule was "If you're not married, you're not loveable."

So, if she stayed married, no matter how bad the relationship, she felt loveable or at least had the chance to be loveable. If you can imagine twenty of these rules running your life, or a hundred, many of them contradictory, then you have an inkling of how little awareness and control we have unless we sort them out and get rid of the bad ones. Rules can be as sinewy and intertwined as a plate of spaghetti or as simple as a three-word sentence.

I created one of the simple ones when I was growing up near Detroit, the "Motor City." In my unconscious, the rule was three words: "Men know cars." Therefore, for me to become a man, I had to learn about cars. I paid attention when my dad worked on the family car Saturday mornings and studied about styles, models and makes, engine size, and what all the numbers and letters on a tire sidewall meant. I proudly stuck out my scrawny nine-year-old chest when I accompanied my father to a tire store one day. As soon as we walked through the door, I spewed out to the man behind the counter all the information necessary to replace our balding tire, surprising the heck out of my dad and the clerk.

Do you have any idea how many buried rules run your life? Lots. Find out how many you have by asking your spouse or close friends willing to be honest. What they have been putting up with may surprise you. You will enjoy ridding yourself of them (the buried rules, not your spouse or helpful friends).

EMOTIONAL RULES

So far, the elements of your roots I have described sound like decisions, "I want to be like Mom" or "become an engineer and build tall buildings." These rules are strong and control our thoughts and actions in many situations and over long periods of time. However, the most powerful ones are not thinking rules but feeling rules. These rules are a product of experiences that affect us on deeper emotional levels. A simple example comes from an event that happened to one of my clients.

One evening, Ted, a twenty-eight-year-old single man, was sprawled on the living room floor of his ground-floor apartment watching a late-night movie when sleepiness overtook him. About ten minutes after he went to bed, a speeding auto crashed through the living room window, ran over where he had been lying, and ended up in smoke and a deafening roar as the tires kept spinning in his kitchen. That was quite a trauma of noise and smoke and what might have happened had he stayed to watch the end of the movie.

For about three weeks, as nighttime approached, he had a sense of anxiety in his stomach, his muscles tightened, and he felt afraid. His emotions were concocting the rule that "Evil lurks in the dark of night" or something like that. What he suffered was a trauma-induced phobic reaction. His feelings created a new rule for him to be on the alert for danger when night fell.

The horrors of a prison camp, a brutal assault, or losing a loved one can scar our emotions for life. Less severe but constant long-term stress can do the same thing. A sudden shock or continued pressure can induce significant changes or further embed old rules. Some of this is psychological and some neurological.

Each of us has an area in our brain called the limbic system. It is an interconnected collection of different brain areas, like a complicated telephone switchboard, that contributes to our experience of emotions. Also, the limbic system has connections to and from the thinking part of our brain, the cerebral cortex. Each of us has a feeling brain and a thinking brain, the two brains are connected, and that connection causes problems.

For Ted, after the car smashed through his window, his feeling brain associated darkness with the life-threat of another car crash.

Let me portray a subtler kind of rule the feeling brain can create. A mother and her four-year-old son Tommy go for a walk each afternoon. Their path takes them by a fenced yard enclosing a small white dog that runs along the fence leaping and barking. Just before reaching this yard, the mother tenses, grabs her son's hand and hurries him across the street. Once past the dog, they return to their original path. What kind of rule do you think the boy's feeling brain is creating?

Depending on his perceptions, he may become fearful of dogs, of white dogs, of crossing streets, or of going on walks with Mom. Whatever it is, the rule becomes how he defines the world and his place in it.

Besides what happens in your life, your interpretation of the event is important. An event can be unimportant now yet significant in two weeks or in twenty years. Tommy's emotional rule might evolve into: "Life is full of dangers."

Or, instead of learning that white dogs are scary, our boy

might grow up feeling that "Without Mom, I'm helpless to protect myself." How about a rule like that running your life? These rules distort your perceptions of the world and yourself, like viewing the world reflected in a wavy sideshow mirror.

Your roots include these mental and emotional rules created by interpreting your experiences. Once these roots dig in, they can forever affect how you perceive yourself and your life. Some rules are simple and silly, others deep and unmovable. You can identify, evaluate and change these pieces of your roots.

CULTURAL AND RELIGIOUS RULES

Imagine you are sitting on the sandy bottom of a wide, slow-moving river. The water, up to your waist, is as comforting and soothing as a warm bath. Stop for a minute, close your eyes, and visualize yourself sitting in the water. You feel the river pushing on your back, flowing around you, and tickling your skin.

Now imagine pushing the river with your hands to make it go faster. What happens? You make waves and create a disturbance, but the river keeps its own pace. Your culture is like a river. It flows slowly yet strongly, carrying much with it. If you oppose this flow, you create a disturbance, but the river continues to flow past you to its destination. Culture is a very strong but slow-moving force.

Your culture taught your parents how to raise you. Or, if your parents were "counter-culture," it told them what to counter. Second only to biology, culture, including religion, is the core of your roots. These rules have evolved over thousands of years yet some of these rules can change quickly, like today people living together instead of getting married or deciding to become a nonbinary gender. Rigid or evolving, cultural rules are massive and have the strength of a billion voices.

We are all subject to cultural rules no matter what our culture. Katsumi Ono, a housewife who lives just outside Osaka, is a prime example. Her two children attend one of the best high schools in the district and receive extra tutoring six days a week. For twenty years she was the dutiful wife and mother her culture expected. Mrs. Ono was a *sengyo shufu*, a stay-at-home wife whose responsibility was to her husband, her children, and her home. She performed her tasks well and was honored in the community. Her husband, unfortunately, was laid off from his job. Bills came due and went unpaid.

To make ends meet, Mrs. Ono had to find work. Too ashamed to go to the local job center, she traveled by bus nine miles to a similar job center in another neighborhood. Once she found a job, she insisted on working nights, so she could continue to keep up appearances. She still performed the same duties at home, making all meals, keeping the rooms clean, ironing her husband's shirts, and bringing him coffee in the morning, but she also worked forty and sometimes fifty hours outside the home. Katsumi didn't have time to meet with her friends, but she was too ashamed to see them, anyway. She woke up each morning ashamed at her family's plight and ended each day exhausted and still ashamed. Katsumi did everything she could, yet it was not enough. Reality didn't count. Only cultural values mattered.

Katsumi is like the rest of us. She is driven to meet the expectations of those important to her: her family, her friends, her neighbors, her culture. Yet no matter how hard she works and how much she accomplishes each day and each week, it is not enough, it will never be enough. Individual accomplishments, no matter how grand they may be, are measured against cultural expectations.

The reason your roots grow so deep is that the basic

function of cultural rules is to ensure the survival of the group, not you, the individual. What this means is your personal life will be shaped to support the group: your needs and goals will take a back seat to group needs. Wars are waged, and mostly young men fight in them because of cultural rules. Although cultural rules can lead to individual tragedy (for instance, in some places a woman who has an affair with a married man can be stoned to death), society as it ages gains a vast amount of wisdom of what works in the long run. We, as short-term occupants of life, benefit from such a perspective. We don't have to abide by all or even any cultural rules, but they have their value.

Cultural rules give us a sense of belonging. Most of them are simple and straightforward such as starting school at age five, old people being respected (or being disregarded), suicide is an honorable act when you fail or are ashamed, or the opposite, that suicide is the quitter's way out of a tough problem. Cultural rules tell us what is right and wrong.

Such strict, clear guidelines help when most of us would shoot from the hip. The more obvious and general the rule, the easier it is to get a sense of well-being and belonging by following the rule. Well-established cultural rules enable the individual to know what to do and when. If everybody follows the rules, everybody knows what to expect from everyone else. Brides wear white, bad guys wear black. No one is surprised. There is minimal uncertainty and conflict; just what is necessary for the security of the group and the comfort of the individual. When this isn't the case, when individuals don't or can't follow these rules, tragedies can occur, like teenagers murdering their classmates.

Religious rules are like cultural rules and overlap in various ways. Most religions include social rules or behavioral expectations that go beyond the veneration and worship of a supreme being. There are many examples, such as honoring parents, committing to high moral standards, and not coveting another's spouse. These kinds of rules are the backdrop for the person's individual rule development. Or, to continue our metaphor, they are the roots from which each of us grows.

SOCIAL, BIOLOGICAL AND DEVELOPMENT RULES

As we grow up, personal traits complicate the situation. Given that each of us is born as a unique being, how a person's characteristics fit into the social rulebook can create problems. For example, let's say little Tommy grows more slowly than other kids. His friends, teachers, parents, and everyone else will respond to him according to their unconscious definition of what this means.

People notice Tommy has deviated from normal and react based upon personal interpretations of these rules. Aunt Hildy, who was short herself, will respond with pity based upon her hurts as a little muffin in the fourth grade. Billy next door makes fun of anyone when he spots a difference because his father makes fun of him all the time. Long-tall Sally, Billy's older sister who plays center on her high school basketball team, envies the kid when she can't get a date. All these reactions are based on the social, development, and biological rules of the standard growth curve that makes height differences noticeable in the first place and then are based upon each individual's interpretation of what breaking this rule means.

Every junior high school is full of examples: boys who are still boys competing in gym class against young men who shave twice a day, girls and women the same age sharing the same mirrors in the bathroom, and boys leading girls a head taller around the dance floor. You probably can think of a biological rule you didn't follow as you grew up and the difficult consequences.

Cultural, religious, social, and biological rules form the basic roots by which we define ourselves. Others notice and judge us by these standards, adding fertilizer or manure, and we measure ourselves as well.

A blatant biological rule is skin color. Whatever color you were born with is normal. Other colors are something else. This simple, obvious element of your roots has caused monumental problems.

Similar to and part of biological rules are development rules. You are not expected to do in the third grade what should be done in the tenth. In addition, a seventy-year-old is not expected to perform the same as she did at twenty. Age-level expectations seem to be most important at the ends of a lifetime, not so much in the middle. But they are still there. The forty-year-old who has not yet married, for example, is suspected of many, mostly negative, personal qualities.

As a culture, we have certain age-rule expectations, such as a ten-year-old cannot drive an automobile and you can't become President of the United States unless you're at least 35. As individuals, we have the same thing: "I can't date until I'm 16" or "I will be successful only if I can retire before 60."

Each family has its own unique set, of strict and not so strict adherence to social rules, misperceptions of social rules, family heritage rules ("A Howell would never eat scrambled eggs smothered in catsup"), parental idiosyncratic rules, and some you make up as you go.

IDIOSYNCRATIC RULES

A parental idiosyncratic rule is a rule learned by the child that arises out of some unique attitude or behavior of the parent. As you know, a child tries to make sense of the world around her and develop a sense of self-identity. If the parent has some peculiarity, the child may assume it's normal and include it in her tangle of roots. Most parents aren't too bad, and their attributes can end up helping the child. For example, a boy whose father was a terrible communicator may better learn how to perceive thoughts and feelings (originally to understand his father), but, later, he may use his sensitivity to become a terrific social worker.

However, as the idiosyncratic becomes more unusual or pathological, the child may need to establish unusual rules to cope. Several of my clients have needed to do this. One, Patricia, had a father who was always cold and distant. He was often rejecting and never told her he loved her. Patricia never married and still visits her father every afternoon to help with errands and chores and to prepare his dinner. She made up a rule that still guides her life: "I will do whatever it takes for my father to finally love me." Adult children of alcoholics are often victims of parental rules gone sour, which can cause significant damage to the family for generations.

Limiting rules can arise from normal parents. Loving, supportive parents can produce a child who learns to follow the rules and is eager to do so, always doing what he is supposed to do. As an adult, even in the middle of the night with no cars on the street, he will wait for the "walk" message on the signal light. For when he was good, he was rewarded; when he was bad, given either the appropriate discipline or taught the right way. This could establish the rule "If I'm good, everything will be peachy," creating a Caspar Milquetoast, a goody-two-shoes, or the fellow standing on the dock waiting forever for his ship to come in.

RULING YOUR ROOTS

To better understand roots, it might be a good idea to

look at them from a different angle. Imagine the Bill and Melinda Gates Foundation awarded you 75 billion dollars to create an experimental new country on Toagago, an uninhabited island in the South Pacific. It wouldn't be a large country, the island can hold maybe 100,000 citizens, but it would be your baby. What would you do?

Would you appoint yourself president? Maybe even king or queen for a time?

Would you opt for a democracy, hoping the new arrivals could figure out the best way to run the new country? Would you like some veto power for at least a little while as things got started?

What about choosing people to populate your country? How would you pick them? Is everyone welcome? Maybe have some entrance requirements, like if you're sick and contagious you couldn't come in or if you had no useful skills you should not apply? Would every religion be welcome including the fringe ones that believe in animal sacrifice? Would you allow in people you know will be dissenters, hoping for the best?

Would you build cities, or would you prefer small villages? Would you want to join the United Nations? Who would be your trading partners?

Who would create laws? How would they be enforced?

What would be the official language?

How long would the normal workweek be?

Medical care for everyone?

How old would people have to be to vote, drink alcohol, drive a car, get married? Could people who love each other get married, even if they're the same sex?

Would there be a separation of church and state?

How would you know if your country was doing well? How would you measure that: opportunities, freedom of the press, gross national product, percentage voting, number of political parties, literacy rate?

How much land would you set aside for national parks?

Would you provide social security?

My guess is that your country would look like where you live now, but with maybe a few tweaks here and there.

What if Bill and Melinda gave 75 billion dollars to another person, someone who lived 10,000 miles from you? Would that person's country be different? Which one would be better?

That last question is a tough call. The countries would be different, that's for sure. The two countries would have different roots, ones each of you created from your own roots. Most people would say that the countries would be equally good countries, but only if measured by a different value scale. They would not be equally good if both were measured by what you considered of value or if both were measured by what the other person considered of value.

Whose roots are the right roots? Whose roots are the best roots?

You are an accident of where and when you were born. Had you been born in a different time and place, you would be different, you wouldn't be the same you. Would that different you be a better you or just a different you? How many yous could there be? Could you somehow collect the best parts of all the different possible yous and be the absolute best you? I think you can.

For your sense of well-being, you rely on the sanctuary of your roots. With them, you gain the wisdom of the ages, but at the cost of them defining who you can be.

Strong roots are good for the individual, to a point. Your roots are monumentally widespread, extraordinarily old, and colossally powerful. But, as they operate now, are they right for you?

Q and A

Are roots good or bad?

Both, but because it is rare for people to examine and reject any or a major portion of their roots, they can turn out to be bad in the sense they keep you in place—a place you didn't choose.

For example, traditions and other elements of your heritage prompt you to behave in well-defined ways that are no longer useful or necessary but are important, anyway. Some Native American tribes, for instance, find it necessary to harpoon whales. They don't need the meat or blubber or oil, but they need to kill whales to define who they are. It's unfortunate any group needs to do harmful things to feel connected to their heritage.

How are roots good?

They connect you with all that came before. They give you a solid base to grow from. They tell you who you are. The downside is that too many people use them to define who they can be, and perhaps just as bad, who others are and can be.

Should I get rid of all my roots?

No. One of the most profound and important feelings for a human being is a sense of belonging. From Mormons to Marines, individuals enjoy membership in a greater force than themselves. Without this, an individual suffers a constant sense of uncertainty. For example, the religion in which we are raised can make all the difference in our sense of our place in the world and eternity. Without roots, we may as well be drifting in space. The idea is to not blindly accept your roots but to consciously decide what is right for you. This is not an easy task.

What should I do about my roots?

Examine your life and identify areas that don't seem to be working well. For example, relationships. See if you can determine if your roots are making trouble. Maybe they're pushing your aim too high or too low. You could be expecting too much. Check many areas of your life and discuss roots with others. Your potential partner might have differing roots. If you find a bad rule, make up a new one and try it out. And, repeat as needed. Also, talk with friends about roots. This will help you develop skills in identifying and pruning your roots.

What should I conclude about my roots?

Roots are a wonderful starting point for the great adventure that is life.

LIFE SKILLS I

Independence

Independence

*Good is strict,
while
evil seems to
arrive carrying a
lovely gift.*

The first element of personal wisdom is independence; independence from your roots and the wind. It will be a constant struggle for most of us because our roots are deep, and the wind is a never-ceasing force in our lives. We must always be learning and fighting our roots and the wind to be independent. Sometimes it may seem as if we must scorn God, disrespect our parents, or condemn society to become independent.

Martin Luther declared his independence when he nailed his 95 theses on the Wittenberg Castle Church door in 1517, freeing himself from what he considered dogma and beginning the reformation.

Rosa Parks did the same with Jim Crow laws when she

refused to give up her seat for a white passenger in Montgomery, Alabama in 1955.

In our own way, at our own level, we all must declare our independence and do it often.

Back when we were kids, my younger brother and I would walk to Sunday school every Sunday. My older sister, with her friend Cherrie from across the street, would attend real church services an hour later. I assume my parents stayed at home reading the Sunday paper and drinking coffee. They gave me a quarter for the collection. My brother had a dime. Every Sunday we'd take the walk along five or six suburban blocks and past a park. I can't recall how old I was, somewhere in the early two digits, when it occurred to me my brother and I didn't have to walk all the way to church. We could play in the park for an hour and then go home. We could spend our respective 25 cents and 10 cents later, on comic books and candy.

The only hurdle would be my brother's tendency to blurt out what should be a secret like he did one Christmas when he told my sister he wasn't supposed to tell she was getting a watch. I swore him to secrecy one Sunday, and we did the deed. Play in the park for an hour, and, pockets heavy with cash, head for home. All that day I waited for the inevitable consequences. The Sunday school teacher would call to ask about our absence. Someone would stop by saying they saw us playing in the park. My mother would notice the poorly brushed off dirt and grass on our clothes. God would somehow alert my father. Or, most likely, my brother would spill the beans. None of those happened.

So, from then on, we made it a practice to head for the park. Sometimes we went to a store; other times explored the neighborhood. Occasionally we went to Sunday school just to keep up on current religious events. We went. We didn't go. It was up to us. This secret escape from Sunday school was one of my early discoveries of independence.

Growing up, at least until that fateful Sunday, like every kid I accepted the rules of my roots as to how the world worked, and I believed that is how the world should work. The wind, in the guise of parents, teachers, and neighbors and in the form of William Boyd as Hopalong Cassidy on TV, kept me clear on what was right, good and expected. After about age eight, things began to get more complicated. Shades of gray emerged out of my black and white world. This happened to you too, maybe earlier, maybe later. The combination of increased self-knowledge and more awareness about the world began to erode the old rules. You and I could no longer simply follow the rules; we now had choices.

The big questions are what rules should you continue to follow, what rules should you ignore, and what new rules should you create.

As you know, cultural rules are for the continued well-being of the group. Some of them, like religious ones, are also for the individual. These rules enable the individual to live in harmony with others and live a moral life.

They do this by defining the behavior or viewpoint for various situations. A universal example is the Golden Rule: Do unto others as you would have them do unto you. This gives you a basic way of approaching people and handling situations. For most of us, we try our best to do this but sometimes fall short. When we fall short, another rule must take precedence. A rule like "Nobody will make a monkey out of me" might just prompt you to "Do unto another before he does unto me." Cultural rules are basic, but they can be ignored or adjusted.

By mid-childhood, the perception of an event becomes as important as the event itself. When I had that extra 25 cents in my pocket, there was more to deal with than just skipping Sunday school. Was I stealing money from God? Was it worse to use that money for candy (in those days enough for five Snickers bars) than to combine it with allowance money to buy my mother a nicer birthday gift? What if I gave that money to a less well-off friend who needed the money to go to the matinee? My friend, one element of my wind, would say such charity was a positive decision. Even my mother, a substantial part of my personal wind, might find the charitable portion of my behavior okay.

As you grew up, you used the wind to interpret what to do and make sense of daily events. Your roots and the wind altered what you could perceive. The wind became more important than reality. For example, people can be optimists or pessimists and distort events. Sally might get a "C" on a test and decide that she'll never learn math. Sue might get a "D" and decide that she will learn more math than anyone. Painful experiences can crush the heart of one person while making another try harder.

Each of us has our own version of what is important and how the world should be. But remember, no matter how logical, realistic, and righteous your point of view may seem to you, it is based on your roots and the wind. Each town, region, state and country, each age level and each sex all have collective perceptions too. As you get older, when you move, when you change jobs, or when you get married, be aware of new rules and how your old rules may impede enjoying your new life. Your possibilities depend on your awareness of how the wind affects your roots and what kind of impact it has on perceiving options and considering other possibilities.

In graduate school, I first knowingly sat next to a homosexual. I was uncomfortable. I didn't know why this situation bothered me. Intellectually I understood the guy, but because of my roots and the wind, I thought he was an affront to normal human beings.

My rule from middle-class upbringing must have been "gays are strange perversions of masculinity and unlike me." I had never met one (that I knew of anyway) and knew nothing about gays and their lifestyle except what I had read in books, yet my response was visceral and negative. Over time and with multiple interactions, my rules evolved, and gays became simply people; imagine that.

The more you know of these social forces and the more you create your own set of rules, the more you add to your personal wisdom. You gain wisdom with each independent decision. You gain wisdom with mistakes, with sharing your point-of-view, and with every attempt to be true to yourself.

Gaining independence isn't easy. If it were, there would be fewer sullen teenagers slamming doors, and many more frustrated parents sleeping the entire night. To go into greater detail to understand the powerful influences of your roots and the wind, look at the Personal Truths section at the end of the book.

Take care every day to ensure you are in charge of your life. It will be easy to assume too much and stay trapped in old ways of thinking, as you may have done wrestling with the riddle of the guy and the glass of water. Unless you know your assumptions, you'll never figure out that the guy wanted to drink the water because he had the hiccups.

Your Brain

Biology gives you a brain. Life turns it into a mind.
Jeffrey Eugenides

Your brain is the most repository of your roots. It has evolved over millions of years for two purposes, to keep you alive and to help you get your genes into the gene pool. Because of that evolution, your brain is twelve thousand years out of date.

About 10,000 BCE, our ancestors were hunters and gatherers, living in dangerous conditions. Their brains were well suited for survival. Reflexes were quick to attack or run from danger. Mental speed to comprehend and respond to threats improved survival chances, as did caution and defensiveness. What was unknown or different instilled fear and distrust. We still have that brain. Researchers at Cal Tech and elsewhere have found neural networks in the brain that monitor environmental uncertainty. The greater the uncertainty, the greater the fear and anxiety.

Beginning 12,000 years ago, the development of agrarian societies created stability; campsites grew into villages, then towns and cities. Our species moved away from direct interaction with Mother Nature into what we have today; most of our daily interactions are with people, not the land or the sea or dangerous wild animals. The problem is our brains have not kept up with the demands of our new environment. We experience a primitive fear reaction to people who look different. We fear people who talk differently. We fear people who act differently. We fear people who disagree.

*   *   *

Your goal is for your brain to be an asset and not a liability in this new people-centric environment. You must update your brain so you can interact with others in the most positive and effective ways. The *Skills* sections will help you do that.

Make sure you learn the difference between what you want and how to get it. Later, you will learn a five-step problem-solving process that will slow down your ancient, paranoid, trigger-happy brain.

Worthiness*

The more you give worthiness, the more you have yourself.

L iving things have worth, a value because they are alive. Many people insist all living things have equal worth: whales, spotted owls, ants, redwood trees, skunk cabbage, slithering snakes, and big old blackbirds. You and I have worth because we are alive and because we are human. We humans have potential, culture, a rich history, achievements, power, and compassion.

There is a related human value. Unlike worth, this one can vary every day, yanked up, down and sideways. It is our personal sense of worthiness. Your inherent worth may be unchallenged, but you have experienced days when your

---

* I am indebted to professor George Vlahos for teaching me this idea.

personal worthiness was as big and solid as Mount Everest, or as small and meaningless as rabbit droppings. People beaten down by life, abused and hurt, can lose all sense of worthiness. It's like hammering a nail, each blow lowers us a notch or two. After a while, our worthiness sinks out of sight, and our sense of worth disappears, too.

On the other hand, an "A" on a test, being told, "I love you," or "That was a super job you did," being accepted at a good college, all can boost our sense of worthiness.

The highest human achievement is to feel worth separate from worthiness so that day-to-day events have no effect on self-value. This occurs when you give up your individuality to a higher calling, like a Gandhi or a St. Francis of Assisi.*

Becoming a saint, however, is beyond the scope of this book, which is geared only toward a life perfect for you. Here, we'll focus on day-to-day worthiness so you can control the effects of outrageous fortune and faux friends.

Rock stars, famous athletes and movie idols suffer worthiness dysfunction in grand proportion. With fans worshiping every move, adulation is theirs every waking moment. They are caressed with praise that has nothing to do with who they really are. All this attention doesn't penetrate more than skin deep. They absorb the faux nourishment and day by day have true worthiness sucked out.

Here's a thought from someone who should know, Abd-el-Raham, who was the Caliph of Cordoba quite a few years ago.

> I have now reigned above fifty years in
> victory and peace, beloved by my subjects,

---

* This is not the same as totally buying into your roots. The difference lies in the value of the higher calling, the well-being of the individual prior to joining, having other choices and an informed decision to join a higher purpose.

dreaded by my enemies, and respected by
my allies. Riches and honors, power and
pleasure, have waited on my call, nor does
any earthly blessing appear to be wanting for
my felicity. In this situation, I have diligently
numbered the days of pure and genuine
happiness which have fallen to my lot: they
amount to fourteen.

There are three possibilities. One, you can float on the
winds of insincerity and feel good for a while. This means
being hip, being popular, being cool, being a king or queen
of something. The downside is that your real self receives no
nourishment. Two, you can give yourself to a greater cause,
like religion, politics, or the environment. This has a
downside too. You could choose the wrong cause, like say,
Nazism, or maybe you don't want to live your entire life for
one cause. Three, you could contribute to worthiness in
down-to-earth ways. Maybe what Gandhi did on a large scale;
you can do in your own world. Worthiness is partly accepting
sincere compliments, but mostly it's the giving of yourself to
others.

Have you received any compliments this week that gave
you a sense of worthiness? Have you said or done something
to others this week that might have contributed to their
feeling worthiness? You can add to your worthiness by
accepting good wishes from others and giving them out
yourself.

It is important to know how your worthiness works. It
can be valid, or counterfeit. You must nurture your
worthiness by doing worthy things while minimizing the
impact of insincere outside forces.

There are truckloads of quotations about how important
it is to be kind to one another. The "Golden Rule" is not

unique to Christianity. Islam, for example, says that no one is a believer until he desires for his brother that which he desires for himself. Buddhism preaches to hurt not others in ways that you yourself would find hurtful. And Judaism says that what is hateful to you; do not to your fellowmen.

*   *   *

Your worthiness is determined by what you do, especially what you do for others.

Lost your job? Depressed? Lonely? Is your sense of worthiness anemic? Do something nice for someone. Pick up a piece of trash on the sidewalk and put it in the trashcan. Say "thank you" more than usual. Volunteer at any of a hundred different places within a few miles of your house. Contribute to the welfare of others and your sense of worthiness will grow tenfold. You'll like who you are, and you'll like your life. Worthiness is yours when you are doing what has value.

Life Values

Values create meaning. Meaning creates a life of value.

You are unique in all the world and for all time. That makes you significant. You number today in the billions. That makes you part of something larger like a word is part of a poem. Being significant and being only a cog in a giant wheel of someone else's design is not easy.

Here's how you do it. Accept that you know little and value everything you know. Accept that you are not in charge and life cannot be fair. To design a successful and fulfilling life, you must have independent awareness; of yourself, other people, the world, and for what you want to do.

Spend time thinking about your place in the universe and what you would like your existence to mean.

DEATH

I'm sitting in a surgical waiting room at the community hospital. This is the place for people waiting to find out how a relative or friend's surgery is going. It is a small square room about fifteen feet on a side, dimly lit, with sparsely upholstered wooden chairs lining three walls. Nervous, solemn-looking people fill all the chairs. I'm one of them. My mother has been in surgery for almost three hours and it may be another three hours before I learn how she is doing. I'm worried and aware of my father's fear as I look at him, so frail and alone in this crowded place. Others are in the same concerned state: moving about, exchanging small talk with the lady volunteers, leafing through old magazines, trying to be confident.

I must do the right thing if the news of my mother is bad. I wonder how I will react. Will I be able to console my dad? Will I cry on the phone when I call my wife? How do I tell my sister and brother? And then my mind wanders back to questions like, "What is life all about, anyway?"

Many of my clients have wondered about this, too. "How does life make sense when children are abused, widows are swindled, and the poor freeze and starve in the land of plenty? What is important; love, success, money, power? How do I know if what I'm doing is right?" To help with these questions, I've sometimes asked clients to imagine themselves on their deathbed at the ripe old age of ninety-nine, knowing they have perhaps an hour left. I asked them to imagine the feelings they might have as they contemplate the ending of their existence and then reflect on the life they lived, what made them feel content, worthwhile, and productive. I asked them to look at what they valued.

I took my own advice. This is what I wrote for my first two values from my deathbed reminiscence.

1. To have touched someone and to have been touched.
2. To have done something meaningful.

Take time to reflect on yours.

LIFE

Another way of looking at values is that they are what get you up in the morning. Much of the time people struggle out of bed because they have to go to work or get the car fixed or take the dog to the vet. We all get up best in the morning when there is something we really want to do, like plant the garden, play tennis, attend a concert, or hold somebody's hand. Would you include this sort of thing in your values? They may not be significant in the grand scheme of things, but they are significant to you.

In his book, *How to Get Control of Your Time and Your Life*, Alan Lakein talked about priorities—doing those things that are most important first. He suggested leaving less important things to last or never getting to them at all. That's what I say too. Your values are the things you want/need to do with your life, so get to know them and get them done.

Remember that a life value is the worth you place on what you have chosen to do. There is no worth unless you make it so. Your list should be what has the most value to you and not something from your roots or the opinion of others.

Your list contains those things you place the most worth upon, the things you prize above all else to be worthy of your time, your efforts, and your caring. This is the most important area for you to understand and do well. It is the reason you exist and the reason you get out of bed in the morning. Let these values percolate in your subconscious from now on.

*   *   *

Why don't you identify your values as soon as you can? Imagine you are very old and lying comfortably on your bed at home, sensing that the end is near. No one is with you, but you are not afraid. Friends and family are close by, talking quietly in another room. You welcome the chance to be alone and look back on a life soon to be over. Imagine what you would think about. Discover what is important.

From this perspective, you will get a better idea of what is important now and in the future. Go lie down on your bed and think about these things. Don't just sit there and pretend to lie down. Do it. Think over your life

You can list these values in the first part of the Personal Truths section at the end of the book. Look at your values again. Are there others you should add? Values should include things such as meaning, happiness, joy, success, excitement, achievements, fun, significance, other people, your environment—everything you think is important.

Have your values changed since you were younger? Should your values change? Check your deathbed list, change any you want to, and list your current ones in order of priority, most important first.

The *Hows* of Values

If your life doesn't surprise you once in a while, you're not doing it right.

When people think outside the box, they are able to look at things outside the framework everyone else uses. Here is a way to do that. To think in a new way, outside the box, know what to put inside the box.

What is inside the box; what you want to accomplish. However vague or detailed that is, what you want to accomplish goes in the box and nothing more.

Outside the box is everything else. Thinking outside the box is being able to separate *what* you want to accomplish from all the various *hows* to accomplish it.

This is what creativity is all about and is what enables you to be independent and develop personal wisdom.

Most people attach what they want to accomplish with

how they will accomplish it, making it impossible to create new ways of living.

Creativity is the ability to let go of the usual and discover new *hows*. By putting only what you want into the box and not how a universe of options opens outside the box.

For example, if what you want is to enjoy a trip to San Francisco, how you do that can be by visiting Fishermen's Wharf, riding a trolley, joining a city tour, any way you choose to value the experience.

What you want to accomplish, the goal is different from all the methods, the *hows*, available.

Whats and *hows* in action are difficult to grasp so I will explain with an example.

My primary value is to connect with others. That's the *what*. This value is very important with my parents. I wanted them to know I loved them. When my mother became ill, and it was clear she needed an operation, the family had to face her past heart trouble and the possibility she would not make it through another surgery.

So, the *whats* for me were her knowing I love her, fear her death, don't want her to die, and letting her know how much she means to me.

As you may imagine, there are lots of ways (*hows*) to do this. There are direct ways, like telling her I love her, or I'm scared about her surgery.

There are indirect ways too. Since some of my ethnic roots are I should not express feelings directly and being a man means suppressing emotions, I sometimes succumb to indirectly expressing the feelings I have for her. I invite my parents to dinner, hug them a lot, ask my mother to make me lunch, and a host of other things we both know express our mutual feelings. Being Dr. Brown also made me an expert, so I could tell her not to worry and that she would be all right. This lent emotional support and allowed our touching in a different way (i.e., her pride in "my son the doctor" and the fulfillment of many of her root-based definitions about being a successful mother).

The *what* was my mother hearing the message that I loved her. The *how* was the method(s) I used; those most comfortable to me and my set of rules and those I thought she could receive, given her set of rules. (My mother, like many of her generation, had a large mass of unexamined roots.)

Another *what* and *how* is this book. My value of doing something meaningful is the *what*. One *how* is by writing a book to help people live fulfilling lives. Other *hows* could be teaching classes, volunteering, or donating to worthy causes.

SIMPLE BECOMES COMPLEX

The clearer the whats and hows of your value system, the easier it is to live your values and reach important goals. Let me explain how it can get complicated. I practiced sports psychology early in my career, helping athletes achieve their best performance.

One professional golfer came to me with the problem of not playing well enough the first two days of a tournament to qualify for the last two days when money is won. It's disheartening to call yourself a professional at something when you're not making any money doing it.

As we first talked, the primary value in this situation seemed to be, "I want to be a successful professional golfer." This was the *what*. The *how* was by "winning enough money to support myself on the golf tour." Simple. Right? No.

Although the goal was to be a successful pro golfer, this *what* was a *how* to gain another *what*: self-esteem. The primary value was "I want to like myself," and the *how* to "like myself" was by being a successful professional golfer. For this athlete, not winning money at a tournament was not just a poor job as a golfer, but a measure of personal inadequacy.

We found that a basket full of rules about self-esteem affected his golf performance. Let's look at this in detail.

A rule (part of his roots) the golfer learned from his parents was, "Things are good or they're bad." This fellow could be playing well, hit a couple of poor shots and figure there was no point in trying anymore—things were "bad." By giving up he accepted the validity of his parental rule and also kept a shred of self-esteem by thinking, "I gave up because fate was against me. Next time, I can do better." This kind of logical assumption we can term a "self" rule, a personal rule of thumb to be used as mortar between other rules. These rules are little gems that a person makes up, is told and remembers, or learns somewhere and decides they are true.

Here's a short list of the professional golfer's rules:

1. I want to feel good about myself.
2. Professional athletes are held in high esteem.
3. If I'm a professional athlete, I feel more self-esteem.
4. Things are either good or bad.
5. A few bad shots means that things are bad.
6. If I quit trying when luck is against me, I can save myself for next time.
7. If I'm a pro, I will be held in high esteem
8. If I'm a pro, I can feel OK.

Like the young lady who needed to be thin to feel in control and thus feel good, our golf pro went through a lot of wiggling around in his rules to feel an adequate amount of self-esteem. Once we understood *what* he wanted, we found easier and more effective *hows* to feel good about himself. We could separate the *whats* and *hows* of being a good human being from the *whats* and *hows* of being a good golfer.

This was important for his self-esteem and his golf. Now tournament performance no longer meant he was a good or bad human being. He gained self-esteem (what) by enjoying the company of others (how) and by trying his hardest to succeed (another how).

He ended up doing better in tournaments (his professional what), by trying his best, getting fully prepared before each shot, and by being more realistic in his goals (much more effective hows for playing good golf).

Everyone does this every day. If what we want is to read a good book, how we choose the book is to ask friends, read reviews, look for a likable title in the bookstore.

If what we want is a new car, how we decide can vary. We can choose by what our father used to buy, by popularity, safety, looks, any number of things. If what we want is a drink, how we make a choice can be by habit, convenience, cost, anything.

*   *   *

It is important to examine your values and how you will achieve them. Remember that almost always, values can be achieved in different ways and if you have only one way, you are probably stuck in your roots.

You will get more out of life if you keep your options free rather than doing whatever your roots tell you to do. Make sure you are defining the right life values *for you* and then explore the best ways for you to achieve them. You must be sure you are heading to the right place in the right way, which, of course, is your way.

Avoiding Someplace Else

If you don't know where you're going, you might end up someplace else.
Yogi Berra

To avoid ending up someplace else, this section presents six assumptions we'll call rules because they have a lot of power and you can add them to your personal wisdom.

These rules will help you overcome your roots and add to your independence. If you accept them (you don't have to) and make them a part of you, you will be hacking away at your roots. The last rule is in the form of a story.

THE SEVEN BILLION RULE

At the time of publication, there were about seven billion individual human beings alive in the world. That is a very large number. Many are poor and hungry, under-educated, without jobs or with little sense of worth, but they're like you and me in all the ways there are to be human. Given the right circumstances, any of them could be another Shakespeare, a Curie, a Churchill, anything. A few of the seven billion are rich, jetting from winter retreat to summer compound, some are content just to make the house payment, while others don't even bother with rent. There are Nobel laureates, movie stars, clerks and carpenters, spendthrifts and penny-pinchers, crooks and saints. None of them sees the world as you do.

You are unique, now and for all time. Your perceptions are the most valid. Your vision is the true understanding of the universe. Your life is wonderful and special. Your point-of-view is the correct one: Along with seven billion, six hundred and ninety-nine million, nine hundred and ninety-nine thousand, nine hundred and ninety-nine other equally good ones. There is no second-best point-of-view.

Everyone is different, yet everyone was born with the same human worth. Your ultimate value as a human, however, is what you do with your unique life.

The Seven Billion Rule says that what you think and feel is valid, and what other people think and feel is also valid whether or not they agree with you or you with them.

Another element of the Seven Billion Rule is this: "At first; everyone; will always; see everything; differently." If everyone is different, it is safe to assume that when faced with a problem or opportunity, or some other choice, everyone will define the event differently until they can exchange information and form a joint perception.

The rule is useful when people gather to discuss an issue and agree to listen to each other before acting from their own point of view.

THE ICEBERG RULE

Icebergs have only a small percentage of their volume above the surface of the water. The greatest mass of an iceberg lies hidden beneath the surface. In that way, people are like icebergs, even to themselves.

Let's say the average human being has a thousand interactions and experiences each day. Some are experiences like feeling tired when the alarm goes off or having a near car accident on the way to work. There are nice things, too, such as enjoying a tasty beverage or bowling a 200 game. All these events combine to make your day unique and contribute to what you are.

Yet, each of these thousand daily life events has a different level of intensity and meaning. They don't all register on the brain the same. Major events, such as winning the lottery or the death of a spouse, have far-reaching impact, whereas running out of shoe polish may not have any consequences at all. Of these thousand experiences, some can be disregarded by the brain and quickly are; others must have their importance multiplied many times to define their effect.

Only a tiny portion of ourselves is in our conscious awareness. The same lack of information holds true, more so, with other people. We have no direct awareness of what is inside the brains of others.

The great majority of what goes on in our own minds, that other 99+% outside our awareness, is comprised of memories, associations, old habits and experiences. It's what Freud and a host of others define as the human unconscious. This part of us is the source of our dreams and fears and is the reservoir of our roots.

This means that you will know only a tiny portion of your thoughts and feelings and the reasons you are what you are and why you do what you do. You know little of yourself and even less about others. This is true for all of us. We are made up of complicated interactions of our rules, experiences, emotions, and interpretations of reality.

There is also a large amount of experimental data that suggest that our experiences affect the physical growth of the brain. Your experiences determine how your neural-brain network is constructed. And, the way your brain is constructed affects how your mind can think, what concepts it can entertain, and what kind of blind spots will exist.

The Iceberg Rule means you don't know a lot about yourself and others, only the most visible part—and that's okay.

It also tells us we should be more accepting of our mistakes and of others making mistakes, to be open to advice and to be comfortable with ambiguity.

THE TWO-CENTS RULE

Early in my career, an odd assortment of people found their way to my office with strange thoughts and fears, some hoping to convince me that Martians were landing in their backyards, others warning me the CIA was poisoning lunches in elementary schools. After talking with them awhile, however, their attitudes and perceptions began to make sense.

I remember a towering and angry middle-aged man, who wore combat fatigues and a leather motorcycle jacket. He also had a large gold earring, a shaved head, and an evil-looking Bowie knife hanging loose in a black leather sheath on his belt. He was tight-jawed and red-faced, agitated, ready to explode, and acted like he just might grab that Bowie knife and slash and stab me into hamburger.

After a few scary sessions, I realized that he dressed like a renegade biker and acted like a crazed murderer because he was afraid. He was afraid of women. He feared that if he fell in love and it didn't work, he would turn to alcohol, become a drunk and die as his father did. As I got to know him, I understood why his fear made so much sense to him and why he used rage to keep people distant. He and I worked together to find a better way of meeting his needs and getting along with women.

The Two-Cents Rule is that most people are working hard to reach reasonable goals and if what they're doing looks stupid, obnoxious, etc., give them two cents worth of credibility until you learn more.

And do the same for yourself. If you've done something hard to understand or made a dumb mistake, give yourself the benefit of the doubt until you figure it out. It will almost always make sense.

THE DECK OF CARDS RULE

You are like the three-of-hearts in the deck of cards of life.

The metaphor is valid in many ways: you are one part of a group, your role and value change according to the game being played and sometimes you are shuffled around by forces beyond your control. But you are a unique individual despite being part of a larger whole. This is important because your definition of the ideal life will be and should be different from everyone else's. It will have elements like others, sure, but it will be specific to your interests, talents, values, experience, and a host of other things.

On the downside, this means that no one will fully understand or appreciate your definition of a fulfilling life, making the whole process a little uncertain and hard to explain. On the upside, it is yours to design and reshape whenever and however you want.

This is a critical idea about independence. No one, not your mother, not your father, not your spouse, not your Uncle Joe, nobody will understand life the same way you do. This may seem to lead to a lonely life, misunderstood by friends and loved ones. But the opposite is true. When you and another share your differing ideas and values, there will be true sharing. There will be no defensiveness, but a mutual experience of learning, growing and connecting to what is most meaningful to each of you.

To stretch this metaphor, imagine the different games you could be in if you were the three-of-hearts. Imagine the number of other cards you could be paired with, the king-of-clubs, the ace-of-spades, even the ten-of-diamonds. What a rich life you would have, relating closely with all types of other cards, experiencing all types of situations and playing all sorts of roles.

Understand that rules and roles are not permanent. Life can change in an instant and change again and again for better or worse. Your best life depends on the choices you make to adjust to change, to create change and to put yourself in charge.

THE REALITY RULES RULE

Life isn't fair. Some babies are born disfigured. Bald preteens die of inoperable brain tumors. A stupid accident claims the life of a father or sister. It rains on your day off. The worst workers (but the best office politicians) often get the promotion and the raise. Medical and telephone bills are nearly always wrong and nearly impossible to fix. Social injustice is a daily occurrence everywhere. You can't fight city hall, you shouldn't spit into the wind, and you darn well better accept that the universe not only doesn't care, it can't care.

If the Seven Billion Rule is valid, it leads to the conclusion that there are seven billion different realities. Although your version is valid, you're wrong to almost seven billion others. (There are at least a few people that would agree with you.) This means that what's fair to you would be out-voted much of the time. In addition, if God is in heaven running things, your version of what is fair may not be the same as how your creator sees the situation. If God isn't keeping a hand on the wheel, then what is fair to you will occur only by chance. What happens is simply what happens.

The universe just is. You just are. Your job is to manage your reality and the rest of the world's reality, so you can remain independent of your roots and accept what is right for you. The more you can create meaning out of all this, the better your life will be.

THE SNAKE RULE (A STORY)

Once upon a time, a traveler happened upon a snake in the road. As it was a cold day in the middle of winter, the snake was nearly frozen and nearly dead. Taking pity on one of God's creatures, the traveler picked up the snake and put it under his heavy coat, hoping the warmth of his body might save the poor animal.

After only a half-mile he could feel the snake stirring under his coat. He smiled, for perhaps his gesture may have saved it. Then he felt a sharp pain. He grabbed the snake and threw it on the ground. In just seconds he could feel the poison seeping through his body.

He looked down at the snake in bewilderment. "Why did you bite me," he asked the snake. "I saved your life."

The snake shrugged its tiny shoulders and replied, "I'm a snake."

The lesson here is snakes will tend to act like snakes no matter what you expect them to be like and they will act like snakes no matter how wonderful your intentions.

*   *   *

To summarize:
- The Seven Billion Rule tells you that you are as important as everyone else, and at first, everyone will see things differently.
- The Iceberg Rule says that you and others are complicated creatures.
- The Two-Cents Rule tells you to trust what you can't yet understand.
- The Deck of Cards Rule reminds you that although you are part of a group, you are unique.
- The Reality Rules Rule and the Snake Rule suggest that it is a good idea to accept that life is not fair, that it cannot be fair, and that your job is to do your best and accept the nature of things with grace and gratitude.

Use these rules to help you become independent.

Personal Goals

*Shoot for the moon.
Even if you miss, you'll
land among the stars.*
Les Brown

Goals do several things: they identify a target, they motivate us to action, they measure progress and they let us know when we have finished our work. On your way to a life that is truly yours, setting goals is like placing milestones to help you measure your progress. Although reaching a goal is nice, being aware of the changing value of a goal also is important.

Remember, our personal rules determine what we see and what we do. Goal setting is useful because it puts into operation our chosen rules and how they combine to fulfill our needs.

Goals tell us what direction to go. For the most part, rules tell us what to do and how to do it. Goals and rules are *whats* and *hows* layered in a series, aimed toward intermediate and ultimate objectives. Knowing how this system operates enables you to control it.

As an illustration, let's observe the rules of the typical weekend softball player. We will separate his *whats* and *hows* and identify goals as we go along. You will be surprised by how what first appears to be a negative situation can be reframed into a positive outcome by understanding rules.

Zack Dempsey, our ballplayer, is settled deep into the recliner in his living room reading the Sunday paper. He's facing the front windows that frame the blue sky of a sweet summer day. A warm breeze slips through the screen door and brushes the soles of his bare feet. Pursing his lips, he recalls what his wife said Friday evening.

"I'd really like you to clean out the garage this weekend."

And like the dutiful husband he was, he promised he would do something with his fifteen-year-old collection of wheel covers and carburetor parts. It was one in the afternoon. There was plenty of time for a pickup game at the park or, sadly, cleaning up his mess. Since he hadn't tried out the new glove his wife had given him for his birthday, he was contemplating the possibility of her understanding another postponement of garage detail.

Goal A: Play softball with the guys
Ah, but Mona (the wife!) wants
Goal B: A clean garage.

Having read the section on *what* and *how*, he thought if he could get a clean garage (the what), by having the kids do it (one of the potential hows), then he was free to play softball and he would check on their work later, after the game. Creasing his forehead, he thought, "Better not."

Goal (and rule) C: Be true to your word.

"What a lousy situation," he complained under his breath. "Just because she caught me in a weak moment, I'm stuck here to clean what isn't all that much of a mess."

"Would you like another cup of coffee, honey?" Mona asked from the kitchen doorway.

He looked at the ogre who had condemned him to the dusty purgatory of the garage, noticing the curve of her hip and the smile on her lips. She looked great. He recalled holding her hand as they'd walked to dinner the night before.

Goal (and one of his most important values) D: Make the woman you love the happiest woman in the world.

I'm sure you know what he did. He compared his whats and hows, figured out the priorities, and did what he wanted to do. He no longer felt he had to clean the garage because he saw it for what it was, a goal, and more importantly, a symbolic gesture (a how) of love. That made it a want-to rather than a have-to.

Get the idea? If you know the ultimate outcome, the real goal, almost any task (how) can be endured. I don't enjoy paying taxes. But I pay my share more easily when I identify two goals: I don't want to be fined and I want to enjoy the benefits of our tax dollars.

THE BIG PICTURE

The key concept of personal goals is to understand what you want and to know the issues and hurdles (mostly your roots and the wind) that must be sorted out. Make sure the issues and goals are yours. Don't make the mistake of comparing your life goals with those of anyone else unless it is to learn something. A personal goal does not have to measure up to the success of someone else's life. You do not have to achieve as much, as quickly, as easily, or anything else that another person has done.

It is easy to fall prey to feeling inadequate when you compare yourself with the best. The success of your life cannot be compared to anybody's. That is one of our human failings and is the primary trap of the wind. But, how do we know if we are doing well at setting goals and if this process is headed in the right direction?

*   *   *

Here are three ways to create personally meaningful goals.

1. Set long-term goals and short-term goals based on your values with concrete ways of how to reach them.

Olympic Gold Medal winners are all goal-setters. Most people have short-term goals: get through the day, relax at home, buy groceries on Saturday. Those who get the most out of life define specific long-term goals, like having two children, retiring at 62, writing a book, painting a picture. Goals that work best have three characteristics:

- Measurable (include time frame)
- Interesting (and rewarding)
- Not too easy (and not too hard)

Goals should be defined as short term, intermediate, and long-term. Having clear goals and methods makes reaching them more likely.

2. Do not rush forward to your goals but enjoy moving toward them.

While you are on your way to reaching goals, notice and take pleasure from the events and activities of getting there. The goal you defined at first may not end up being what you want once you get there. Define goals, enjoy moving toward them and be aware of what's most important along the way.

But don't do only what is important. As you think about setting goals, remember that the simple feeling of contentment is a worthwhile goal. So are naps, fishing, listening to music, learning to moonwalk, and watching a Laurel and Hardy movie. Achieving something important or significant is not the only kind of goal. Enjoy yourself during the time you have.

3. Improve each day.

This idea is taken from management practices and sports, where the emphasis is on continuous improvement. We can do the same thing. As you list goals, things you will do, ways to enjoy a sense of worthiness and all the other activities of living, try to do just a little better today than you did yesterday. You can do this by taking that extra step that presents itself each day.

Hold open a door for someone or sign up to give blood when you never have before. Do one more good thing each day, that's all it takes. Stretch your boundaries. Contribute to the world. Immerse yourself into every moment. Live your ideal life.

Fair

Fair is not equity, it is you doing the right thing.

Third graders hate it when someone gets two pieces of candy and they get only one. "That's not fair," they say. Fairness to children means equality. It also means an equitable return on investment. If a child works hard on a project, the grade received should reflect that effort. It isn't fair if Johnny worked all by himself for seven hours to construct a miniature volcano and gets a "B" when Steve worked only two hours with his Dad's help and gets an "A."

"Fair" is a word for the schoolyard where children are learning about rules. Following the rules to understand fairness is a necessary step in learning responsibility and empathy. We must be sensitive to our impact on others and take responsibility for what we do. However, the word "fair" is not useful after we turn 14.

"Fair" is only a concept. It is not something that exists by itself, nor is it something you can make happen. Like justice, the concept of fair doesn't work as we want it to in the real world. But we can define it so it achieves the results we're after.

You have been given the gift of life. What is fair is for you to give back to life in the best way possible.

When I was growing up in suburbia, my father made me do something unfair. There was no fence between our back yard and the neighbor's, just a telephone pole at the back corner we used as an unofficial boundary marker.

When I mowed the lawn, I cut the grass to the inside of that pole, making sure I didn't cut one blade of grass more than necessary.

My father, however, had a different view on things. One day he noticed what I was doing and ordered that henceforth, I was to mow not only the entire width of that pole but one more cut on the other side to make sure we had done our share.

The first few times I endured this extra work I moaned and groaned about the unfairness of it all. Then, after a time, I got used to the idea. It even felt good. Eventually, I understood the concept and made it a practice to mow that extra row and then one or two or even three more. Quite a few times I cut grass all the way to our neighbor's vegetable garden and more than once, I cut their entire back yard and then even the front yard while they were away at work.

If life cannot be fair, where does that leave you?

Why should you contribute to the well-being of anyone else when they don't contribute to your well-being?

Because when you contribute, you make the world better than it would have been.

*   *   *

Doing your share and a bit more is what's fair. Can you imagine a world like that?

Probability

God does not throw dice with the universe.
Albert Einstein

I often ride the #417 bus to work. It's a big blue and white articulated one, two bus sections held together with a flexible joint in the middle. My seat is toward the back on the right-hand side. It is my seat. I have earned it through thousands of bus rides, waiting at the bus stop in rain, snow and the odd day of sweltering heat that can happen even in Seattle. I have encountered mornings when the bus was late and a few times when the bus didn't come at all. My seat may or may not be the best one, but it suits me.

Sometimes a new rider gets on before I do and takes my seat. On these mornings I'm reminded that I have no entitlement to that seat. I don't have entitlement to anything. This brings us to one of the great lessons in life.

There is little cause and effect in human existence. You

cannot make someone love you. You will not become rich just because you work hard. There are no secrets to happiness. There are no three things you can do that will guarantee your popularity. There is no one best way to lose weight and be healthy. God may or may not respond to your personal requests. Your government may or may not help you after a disaster. The novel you just started may or may not end the way you want it to.

A useful way to understand how to make your way through life is to accept the uncertainty of existence. Every day, there is a chance you will die before lunch. The only certainty is that one day you will become dead. You can't stop that any more than you can control the weather.

When you race through a yellow signal light, you increase the chance of having a car accident. When you work hard at your job, you increase the chance that the business will thrive, and you will receive a paycheck. If you save for retirement while young, you increase the chance of enjoying retirement. Every choice you make increases the chance of something happening.

There is no *only* way of getting from here to there. There is no one right way, and there often isn't a best way. Life is not either this *or* that, but this *and* that. Thinking of your actions as probabilities allows you the independence to choose because they are not actions that worked or didn't work, but actions that changed degrees of probability.

*   *   *

Living your ideal life is not a matter of winning or losing. It is not being right or wrong. It is choosing a direction most likely to get you where you want to be, on your own or with others. You can live your ideal life by being aware of probabilities and doing whatever you can to maximize the likelihood of reaching your goals and living your values.

Living your ideal life is also accepting the reality that no matter what you do, sometimes it will turn out badly. The best you can do in life is to make decisions that increase the probability of good things happening and decrease the probability of bad things happening. And if worse comes to worst, accept the bad things and move on.

Wide-angle Vision

This art of resting the mind and the power of dismissing from it all care and worry is probably one of the secrets of energy in our great men.
Captain J. A. Hadfi

Although the origin of the *Serenity Prayer* popular in addiction recovery is uncertain, the current version attributed to Reinhold Niebuhr suggests a useful concept.

> God grant me the serenity
> To accept the things I cannot change;
> Courage to change the things I can;
> And wisdom to know the difference.

Like many suggestions, however, it tells you what to do, but not how. I have a way you can achieve serenity by accepting things you cannot change. Later, in the *Skills II* section, we'll talk about changing things you can.

In modern terms, a lack of serenity means you're frustrated or stressed-out. Knowing how to live without frustration and how to avoid stress will allow you to achieve wide-angle vision leading to serenity.

Serenity formula: $F = E - R$

This formula means that frustration is equal to the difference between your expectations and reality. An expectation is thinking the world will operate according to your rules. Since you aren't the center of the universe, there will almost always be a difference between what you want and what you get. The more you can match your expectations to reality, the less frustrated you will be and the more you will be creating serenity, an important component of an ideal life.

If you have no expectations, like some Buddhists and others strive to do, you will always be able to accept reality. If you have no expectations, there is nothing to subtract from and frustration cannot exist. Modulating expectations is not that hard to do, with a little practice, anyway. Define a goal and work toward it. Don't rely on reaching it. Work toward it anyway. If you reach it, fine. If you don't, don't dwell on what didn't happen, learn from the experience and move on.

STRESS

What more can you ask of yourself than to try your best, accept reality and go on? Sometimes, though, life just must be endured for a while. When that happens, you must cope with the stress.

Stress is any change in your environment that makes you adjust, from the room getting hotter, to winning the lottery, to having a bad hair day. Overwhelming stress, or stress over a long period, can lead to physical or emotional exhaustion, which is when you can no longer summon the energy to cope. This is when an exhausted zebra succumbs to the pride of chasing lions even though it means death.

There are three ways to respond to stress:

1. Avoid
2. Balance
3. Discharge

Avoiding stress requires planning.

- Hazardous left turn on the way home? Chose a route that will avoid it.
- Hate worrying about work in the middle of the night? Prioritize, complete top ones by the end of the day, the rest can wait or be forgotten.
- Tough phone call to make? Make it first.
- Stress too tough to deal with now? Postpone overcoming it while you try the techniques listed below.

Balancing stress means to create as much positive as necessary to overcome the negative.

- Tough call to make? Promise yourself a reward, make the call, enjoy the reward.
- In a stressful situation? Distract yourself with a thought of how you will reward yourself later or take a pleasurable time-out for a few minutes.
- In a stressful situation? Remember that it will be over, eventually.
- Still in a stressful situation? Divide the stresses

into smaller parts, only so many hoops to go through until you're finished.

Discharging stress can be active or passive.

- Active: Exercise, yell, sing, punch (an inanimate object, not a person or a dog), walk, etc.
- Passive: Relaxation exercises, listen to quiet music, read a good book, focus on the moment.

Serenity is accepting the world, accepting our limited power in the world, and accepting that doing all we can do is enough no matter what the outcome.

* * *

Whenever you feel frustrated, look at both your expectations and the reality of the situation. To reduce frustration, you can reduce your expectations or improve the situation or both. Often, it is your expectations that are the culprit.

The formula also works well when you are dealing with someone who is frustrated, whether it is a customer, an employee, a friend or anyone else. Together, examine their expectations and help them adjust if their expectations are clearly out of bounds. Examine the reality. Can something be improved to make the situation better? Customer service folks do this intuitively. They don't take a complaint personally; they clarify the customer's expectations, analyze the reality, and figure out how to bring the two into balance.

Defining Moments

Bomb Squad leader after cutting the blue wire: "Oops."

I searched, but I couldn't find one universal life concept that fit everyone. Different life circumstances produce different perceptions, needs and desires, and doing your best isn't definite enough. But there was one idea that could fit everyone, from corporate CEO to a street beggar, from prince to pirate, and that's defining moments.

Defining moments are those life events where your true character is exposed and expressed. It is a time when you choose between conflicting values such as "Do I stay in school or go for that great job?" It is a time when you define who you are and what you stand for.

Some people live their lives without ever noticing a defining moment. The average sociopath hasn't a clue.

Robbing a liquor store isn't much different from tossing down a six-pack. Contrariwise, self-absorbed people see every gesture, every thought, every tweet as a celebration of life (theirs in particular). We all know these types, always focused on themselves and their adventures, with every experience validating how wonderful (or unlucky or whatever) they are, and boy, do they tell us everything about it.

Great people are great because they have great defining moments, George Washington at Valley Forge, for example. Important people are important because they had important defining moments like Paul Revere's midnight ride or the average firefighter entering a burning building. Most of us make do with smaller, yet no less personally significant events: accepting a new job, getting married, having a baby, and coping with the death of a friend. In between and all around these milestones are a thousand and one other moments, some we miss, some we don't, many we misunderstand, but each one defines us and our passage through life.

Harold is a mid-level manager in a large company that makes zippers. He is a dedicated worker and has been promoted regularly. Just as regularly, he works late. One afternoon, his eight-year-old son calls, "Dad, can you come to the game after school and watch me?" Harold looks at the pile of papers on his desk. "Can't today, son," he answers. "But I will make the next one."

You know the story. Harold may or may not make the next one, but he shuffles paper at his desk far more than he watches baseball games.

Individually, none of the requests from his son is a significant defining moment, but collectively, they add up Harold's values and display how Harold defines himself, his job, and his son. It's a little like the collective weight of straw that breaks the camel's back. Each decision is minimal and always defensible. The whole lot can cripple the intentions of a meaningful life.

But, none of us can do what we want to every moment. Short-term sacrifices are made for long-term gain. That's one cornerstone of maturity. However, every time we decide, it's another layer of what we are. Like Jacob Marley's heavy chains of remorse in Dickens' *A Christmas Carol*, we forge an identity with every decision. The chains of defining moments we drag behind us can be understood as three types, but with considerable overlap.

SLIPPERY SLOPE MOMENTS

Small decisions, which one by one over time define who we are; we shall call *Slippery Slope* types. No matter how small, each subsequent decision adds consequences. Decisions like driving fifteen miles per hour over the speed limit do a lot of things: increase the probability of an accident each time; provide a bad example for others in the car; and even, in its own small way, mocks conservation efforts by excessive fuel consumption and extra wear and tear on the car. Here are a few examples of *Slippery Slope* defining moments:

- Practicing unsafe sex
- How you respond when a young child is upset
- What you do when cut off by another car
- What you do if you're wrong

DEAL-WITH-IT MOMENTS

Deal-With-It defining moments are those important situations that are thrust upon us. *Deal-With-It* defining moments occur when the background becomes foreground.

These are defining moments we find ourselves in, not those we created.

Let's go back to the zipper company. Susan is a division manager. One day Harold comes to ask for time off to see his son play in a baseball game. Susan is new to the company but savvy. She knows the company is in survival mode. The Better Button Company has taken over many of their best accounts. She also realizes that Harold's needs are the tip of the iceberg; many staff members have pressing personal issues. Being aware that one of the top concerns of employees is having personal needs recognized and appreciated, she has a dilemma; human needs vs. company needs. She didn't ask to be in this dilemma, it's just part of her job. But she is experiencing a *Deal-With-It* moment.

However, this type of situation isn't always a *Deal-With-It* moment. Tom, a manager who is a company man and doesn't realize there are multiple viable options, would spout the company line without a thought, adding to his collection of *Slippery Slope* moments. It's a *Deal-With-It* moment for Susan since she is aware of the conflicting business and human values. Such defining moments can be difficult and hurtful. For example, someone whose parents are ailing and may need to be put in a nursing home faces a personal defining moment and could be creating a defining moment for the aging parents. People facing decisions about their own health often must make difficult life-threatening or at the least quality of life choices.

A few *Deal-With-It* defining moments are:

- You earn the family income in a job you hate and a better, but lower-paying job becomes available
- A co-worker you like is stealing from the company
- You're busy and someone needs a favor
- You find a wallet containing $600

- A casual friend asks for a large loan you can afford to give

GO-FOR-IT MOMENTS

Go-For-It defining moments are those our actions create. If Susan and Harold chuck their jobs at the floundering zipper company and become freedom fighters, finding themselves shooting guns and ducking incoming shells are direct and predictable results of their defining moment.

Some examples of *Go-For-It* moments are:

- Telling someone what you really think of them
- Saying "I love you" when you feel it
- Reaching out to someone in need
- Committing to a cause
- Choosing your attitude when you get out of bed

Your life is made up of hundreds of *Go-For-It* moments and thousands of *Slippery Slope* and *Deal-With-It* moments. Only by being aware of them and knowing how to make the most of each type, can you live a contented, happy, fulfilling life. Too many of us define our moments with invalid assumptions, other peoples' opinions, or don't even notice when the moments have come and gone. The result is that your life is not yours, but only a shadow of what it could be.

This happens for two reasons. Manager Tom is an example of one reason. He sticks to the company line because that's all he knows. He also votes the party-line in every election, buys the clothes the magazines say he should wear, and gets his hair trimmed and the lawn cut every Saturday morning because that's what his dad did.

His defining moments are lost in his roots and the wind. Macho men will always do what macho men do, ladies will always do what is ladylike and boys will always be boys. It's like a school of fish or a flock of birds all changing direction at the same time. There is little or no individual definition.

The other reason we don't do well with defining moments is that when we have one, we rarely have the tools to cope with it or it is too late to do something about it. Freedom-fighter Susan, for example, exchanged her desk for a foxhole and her computer for a rifle. But she desperately missed her children, Sarah and Bobby. She was in the middle of nowhere, worried about her kids, scared, hungry, and worn out. The romance of the revolution was gone. Susan resented the demands of her comrades. She became sullen and withdrawn, no longer of use to the movement but she wasn't doing anything for her children either. Unfortunately, she failed to create a new *Go-For-It* defining moment and suffered a *Deal-With-It* defining moment when a sniper's bullet shattered her spine and she returned home a cripple.

Sometimes we don't recognize that a defining moment is occurring or, perhaps worse, we have no power to create the definition we would like. This leads to remorse, regret, and missed opportunities; a life of "if only." We can do better.

*   *   *

When facing a choice, take time to determine if this is a defining moment and what kind it is. Examine your values. Choose wisely.

Define
Your
Moments

Some are born great, some achieve greatness, and some have greatness thrust upon them.
William Shakespeare

L iving, like any journey, entails coping with what fate brings your way, making adjustments where and when possible, setting goals, taking responsibility, moving forward and not getting in anyone's way while you do, trying your best, accepting the worst, and, as well as possible, doing it your way.

Since you do not exist in a vacuum, you need to consider and respond as best you can to the potholes and ice patches that occur on your journey.

I had a series of tough *Deal-With-It* moments. In both seventh and ninth grade, I had an English teacher who caused me years of shame and embarrassment. Friday mornings this teacher lined up his two English classes on either side of the classroom for a spelling bee. This was great fun for most of his students because it replaced more boring work. It was great fun if you could spell. The teacher further enhanced these carefree mornings by his "board of education"; five smacks for the first student to miss a word, three for the second, and one for the third.

Every Friday morning, I woke up with feelings of dread and a stomachache. Often, I was one of the first three to miss a word and had to walk between the rows of other students to the front of the class, bend over while being held down by the neck and be administered my education. If I was lucky to get it right when it was my turn, I then had to endure the teacher's sarcastic congratulations.

The ninth grade was worse because the teacher hit hard enough to bring tears to the eyes of this young man trying to become an adult. I thought I was stupid. No matter how I did in other classes, this emotional trauma defined my worthiness. It wasn't until I knew about learning disabilities and the reasons I couldn't spell, not until I was in my late twenties, did I realize and trust I was smart.

This all too common situation, trauma at the hands of an insensitive teacher, was a negative life event by which I defined myself for years. There are many such life events, some only spontaneous comments that have a profound impact. A science teacher in high school told one young woman when she was running for class office, "They sure couldn't elect a nicer, smarter, or better person for the job." He said this as an off-hand part of normal homeroom announcements. Not a big deal, yet he gave her the courage to do much more later in life. She remembered his words when she faced other, more difficult challenges.

Many defining moments are more obvious. Marriage or bringing home a newborn are delightful examples. Others are not so good. Some of my clients suffered cancer, strokes, divorce, or bankruptcy. Like all defining moments, they can be defined and coped with in various ways.

*   *   *

Think about some of your defining moments, from four to eight years of age, eight to twelve, teenager, young adult, mid-adult and senior. Some readers will not yet have reached mid-adult. If you are one of those, anticipate a life event you fear happening or would like to occur. This will help with later sections. For those who haven't yet become wizened, imagine one of the following events happening: retirement, chronic illness, success of a child, fatal illness, death of your spouse, or a lifetime achievement award.

A good psychotherapist could make a lot out of what events you listed and your interpretation of the moments. In our own informal way, let's analyze what you have written. I will ask a series of questions and you think of your answers. As a book, I cannot tell you what your answers mean.

If you wish, ask someone you respect about your responses and see what you can learn. One general question to ask yourself is if and how your roots or the wind are involved in your moments and how you defined them. For example, is an event meaningful because it provided something others may have craved, but you didn't?

1. Are your moments all one kind (like all bad, only *Deal-With-It* moments or *Go-For-It*)? If so, how come?

2. Are one or more positive? Do you enjoy recalling this moment as much as you should?

3. Are one or more negative? Are you over them as well as you could be? Why or why not?

4. Do any of them have to do with other people? In a good way? Why or why not?

5. Did you have difficulty thinking of defining moments? How come?

6. What kind of mood did this put you in? Why?

7. Do you see the importance of being aware of the impact of defining moments?

8. Can you compare your defining moments and what they mean to you with someone else's moments, like a friend or a relative and what the moment meant to them?

9. Would you have chosen different dividing lines? How would you have done it?

10. Did you avoid listing a particular moment? How come?

The more you understand your defining moments, the more you can make them what you want them to be.

Now it is time to look at the ultimate defining moment.

Meeting Your Maker

Guilty with an explanation, your Honor.

The ideas you have just explored should help you become independent. Years ago, I came up with a concept that may make doing that easier. In high school, I began each year with a new notebook, clean, neat, unblemished. I bought new pens and pencils. I had folders, paper, markers, everything I needed in pristine condition. By the end of the year, my notebook was filled with notes and doodles, torn by use and stained by misuse, while most of my pens were leaking ink and my pencils were worn to their last inch, if I had any of the original ones left, that is.

I decided one day that these tools of high school would serve as a metaphor for my life. I envisioned a life file, like a student's cumulative record, which at birth starts off neat, clean, and empty, to be filled with the realities of day-to-day living. My original idea was to keep this metaphoric file neat and clean. Neat, clean file. Neat, clean life. When I met my maker, I could hand over a personal history more pristine than any valedictorian's report on rainfall in Honduras. A little thought, however, made me recognize the terrible error I would have made.

The only way to keep my file neat was to avoid making mistakes. The best way to avoid making mistakes was to do only those things endorsed by my roots. My life would have to be spent in ways that had little to do with me. I soon realized that my metaphor was useful only if I envisioned handing my maker a ripped, dog-eared and stained file that represented giving my all to living a full life. A neat file reflects a safe life, one that doesn't have much to it. A terribly worn file, near to falling apart, is symbolic of living life as completely and personally as possible. That's what I wanted to do. A file on its last legs: A life fully lived.

The bottom line? Meet your maker. It's you.

Take responsibility for your brief yet wonderfully significant existence. Make your life yours and, if you can hand over a file of your collected moments to a higher power, make sure it is in bad enough shape to warrant a smile of acknowledgment. Do what makes you proud. Fill your file to overflowing. When you meet your God, feel the need to pause a moment to catch your breath.

* * *

Live so that if you have the chance to stand before God, you're told, "No one did that before. Well done!"

Caring for Yourself

Don't bother just to be better than your contemporaries or predecessors. Try to be better than yourself.
William Faulkner

Maybe forty years ago, my brother-in-law Dan told me a story that stuck in my mind. When he was a kid, Dan spent the late summer on his grandparents' farm complete with an apple orchard, a wide wooden porch and a filled to overflowing apple barrel.

Like most people, his grandparents lived very much by their roots. They would often say, "One rotten apple spoils the rest." And they told Dan he should eat the apples that were going bad before they spoiled all the good ones in the barrel.

Shaking his head and laughing, Dan told me that in all the summers he visited the farm, he never once had a good apple.

Many of us think we care about ourselves, yet we are not

so good at doing it. We never eat that good apple. Rationalizing, postponing, self-bargaining and a multitude of other mental gymnastics often impede our taking care of our needs. The goal is to end every day satisfied with yourself. Here are ten ways you might try to help you do that.

1. Judge yourself honestly, but not harshly.
2. Don't judge others at all.
3. Keep an eye on the future while you live in the moment.
4. Do everything, except smiling, in moderation.
5. Drive your car, eat, drink, and exercise as if your life depended on it.
6. Appreciate kids for who they are and who they can become.
7. Every day do something that challenges you, do something nice for someone, and talk to someone you care about.
8. Gaze at the sky as often as you can.
9. Tell selected others the truth about yourself.
10. Learn to hug really well.

*   *   *

Or, if you wish, make a list that better enables you to live your ideal life.

Q and A

Bob, the ideas for gaining independence were simpler than I expected. But, can you summarize?

Yes. I did my best to give you new, perhaps alternative rules to compare to the ones you operated from until you began to create your own personal wisdom. You can accept them, reject them, change them. All I ask is that you think about them, talk them over with your family and friends, and then decide what changes you want to make in how you operate in the world.

Are rules, roots and the wind the same thing?

Yes, and they are the same as an expectation, a need, obligation, desire, have to, want to, requirement, anything that drives us to do something. There are many forces in life, and you can call them whatever you like. My intent was to help you see you have, and must make, choices in how you live, and the best way of living is to understand how the world works and what is important to you.

If I have understood everything so far and done all the thinking, doing and sharing you suggest, what should I be like now?

You should be excited to learn more, have a closer relationship with your friends, be sensing many examples of your roots every day, and feel you are becoming more aware moment to moment about who you are and the value of what you are doing. You are also changing some of your attitudes and behavior. You might be smiling more too

.

OTHERS

Others

*Does this make me
look fat?*
Anon

Your roots have made you what you are, solid, down to earth, fixed, and maybe stuck. Without roots, you cannot stand, but with deep roots, you cannot move. Your roots are from the lives of everyone before. You were born connected to your roots and created your world out of theirs. As you grew, as your world grew, life became more complicated. You were not automatically welcomed into peer groups, jobs or relationships. New forces began to push and pull at your identity. Outside opinions became critical. The wind is how everyone tries to make you more like them.

The wind is all the forces at work every day trying to influence you including your friends and family, current cultural norms, fads, politics, advertising, celebrities, TV shows, anyone and anything that encourage you to change, including books like this one.

The wind will be in your face, it will push you in the back, and jostle you side to side. Your roots, like an oak tree's, protect you against the wind. Roots are often not enough. The wind can be as deadly as a hurricane or as gentle and pleasant as a zephyr. The wind can take you to places you never imagined, for better or for worse. Your job is to read the wind and adjust in ways that are best for you.

THE GOODE OLDE DAYS

A long time ago, hunting or gathering was how most people spent their day. No one went to the gym to work on their abs. Raising kids to take their place in the group was the main priority after finding something to eat and staying safe. The meaning of life all those years ago was in telling stories as the sun set and shadows crept over the hills and valleys. People lived in small bands and took care of one another. There was division of labor and the beginning of roles, hierarchies of power and prestige and cultural expectations. Here is a little story of how the wind may have been created.

By accident, Short-one's wife Blue Eye discovered fire. It wasn't so much fire she discovered, quite a number of people were familiar with the ribbons of blue, red, and yellow that magically turned into black wind. What she discovered was the wonderful taste of venison after she stumbled and dropped a deer leg into the fire, and later, when the colored ribbons and the finger sucking hurt that accompanied them were gone, picked it out again. She tasted the charred meat, then gave it to Short-one who smelled it and then bit off a chunk. Short-one raved for weeks to all his friends about the wonderful new food while Blue Eye secretly experimented dropping meat into the fire or onto hot coals, even poking a stick through the meat and turning it over and over above the fire until it turned black. She threw in roots, eggs and other ingredients to see what would happen. All of Short-one's friends were envious and wanted this new taste. All Blue Eye's friends were jealous and wanted to know how to make it themselves. The wind began to blow. Measurement of self and comparison to others was born. So was the concept of self-esteem and inadequacy.

Some of Blue Eye's women friends never got the hang of this fire-cooking business. They would burn the meat every time, turning the mammoth roast into charcoal, and soon their husbands left. Others developed skills way beyond Blue Eye and could whip together a medium-rare steak with a side salad, throw a few colorful petroglyphs on the wall for atmosphere, and live happily ever after with the best men of the tribe.

Blue Eye's simple well-done style was no longer nouvelle cuisine, and she eventually moved away. At the same time, the men began competing to bring home the best cuts of roasting meat; tossing spears great distances and with increasing accuracy. Successful hunters enjoyed many wives who were good cooks and were able to father many children.

The men with weak arms or weak hearts, like Short-one now he had become fat, stood on the sidelines, praying for the quick invention of personal computers or at least big, fast cars.

Thousands of years later, women who could ward off evil spirits were elevated to the status of goddesses and worshiped with gifts of rubies and diamonds. Centuries after that, quite a few of these same kinds of women were burned at the stake as witches. Men with strong arms ruled the early tribes, but later, thin-haired men with glasses and sharp pencils took over and musclemen became laborers on the railroad and were put out of work by steel-driving machines.

Peter Paul Rubens portrayed fat as fabulous; Jane Fonda preached that thin was in. A crew cut and a strong jaw made a heroic lady's man in the nineteen-fifties and an insensitive Neanderthal in the nineties. You were hip and in, or square and out.

PERSONAL SATISFACTION

It all sounds silly, doesn't it? When we judge ourselves, try to fit in, envy others, feel inadequate, follow trends, we measure ourselves with a rubber yardstick. What is important and popular seems to be always changing and always demands one more thing. Much of what we value, in ourselves and others, has the longevity of potato salad on a hot summer day. Being able to cook a dead elephant, sporting the right buzz cut, even being the richest person in the world are all pretty much meaningless unless...

Unless what? Unless during and at the end, your life has satisfied you. The only thing of significance is that you feel that your time on this earth has been worthwhile. You are the only one who can say what is of true value and what is not. Your own value comes from what you have done, liking who you are, and being proud of what you stand for. The catch, and it's a monumental one, is figuring for yourself how to assess your life as you go along so you can be satisfied now and at the end, learning and improving along the way.

Wouldn't it be wonderful to arrive in heaven and be able to review the moments of your life, then come back and adjust here and there? Saint Peter would say, "Rest up for a while and take time to reflect. We'll give you a chance to return and correct things before you are judged for entry through the Pearly Gates." What a wonderful opportunity to get everything just so. But wouldn't it be nice to do it right the first time?

Measuring your worth as you currently do, with the rigidity of your roots and the fickleness of the wind, almost guarantees you cannot enjoy the self-esteem you deserve, nor be free enough to live your life to your full potential. You have a thousand and one voices in your head telling you what is good and what is bad. A teacher has convinced you it is wrong to drop out of school. A maiden aunt is proof you must marry before you turn thirty. A dozen voices together tell you that tall is better than short, thin better than fat, and attractive better than plain. Other voices declare that few beautiful women are smart. If one is smart and ambitious, she's also a bitch. Stereotypes, bias, prejudice, assumptions, all stem from expectations you face every day, including what your family and friends believe is right.

One point of view suggests that your life is simply the product of your heredity and environment and that's it. You have little potential for change or improvement. You may as well have been born a grasshopper or a rose bush. A grander view, however, is that you can learn and transform who you are, and each experience can add to your well-being. The key is gaining knowledge of the forces on your life, and perspective of what is true, what is significant, and what is of lasting value.

The Diabolical Duo of your roots and the wind tells you if the world is a good or bad place, who your friends and enemies should be, whether you will be successful and whether you're loveable. They tell you everything you think, feel and believe. Do not run your life according to a version of the truth you haphazardly acquired as a child. How can you expect to be content or successful based upon an eight-year-old kid's idea of the world, a world that no longer exists for you and never really existed? Few people change their basic rules as they get older. What they do is to apply simple rules to more complicated situations like Alice did to find a place for everything no matter what; they continue to see only what the Diabolical Duo allows them to see.

MARY ANN

Mary Ann is sensitive to feelings, is logical, isn't afraid of work, and generally is an all-around delight. She is happily married, has a good job, and is planning a family. So, what's the problem? The problem is that she can't enjoy any of these wonderful things. Sure, she could tell you about them and how nice they are, but they don't feel important to her. The wind stops her from enjoying her husband, her work, her potential, and her life.

When she was young, about seven or eight, she felt that she wasn't quite right. What caused this feeling was an early effect of the wind. It could have been a casual remark by her father that hurt her feelings. Or it could have been that her older sister seemed to be the favored one. The exact cause isn't important.

What happened, though, is that as a developing young woman she watched for signs she was not OK, mostly by being aware of other people's actions and reactions. It wasn't a lot at first. She looked and felt normal as she was growing up but had this vague uncertainty about herself.

Then, one day, this uneasiness, a feeling of "you're not so

hot," leaped into the primary focus for her life. Like most girls (and boys) as they reach adolescence, she worried about how she looked. At this point in her development, she was trying to define herself as an adult. Since this adolescent period is also a time of emotional upheaval, she also was seeking ways of feeling under better control.

Through a series of experiences such as comments about her being pudgy, noticing she felt thinner when she dieted, television commercials extolling the virtues of a slim silhouette, and approving comments from others when she was thin, she learned how to cope with her "you're not so hot" feeling. This is the sequence of rule-making that went on in her head for a few years:

1. I'm not so hot.
2. I'm not in control.
3. I'm fat.
4. People like me when I'm thin.
5. I can control my weight (by eating very little).
6. I will do whatever it takes to be thin.
7. People will notice how thin I am, and I will feel good.
8. As long as I am thin, I am in control.
9. As long as I am in control, I'm okay.
10. I am okay by being thin.

Soon, an all-consuming focus on weight was born.

Notice numbers 1, 4 and 7. They are great examples of the wind (i.e. others' opinions of who we are and what we should do, and even how we should look). It will not be easy for Mary Ann to change this powerful wind because that would give up what has become a sure way of feeling good, which is difficult to do. In addition, giving up this system and just being herself would not elicit such a rewarding feeling for her as someone saying, "My God, you're thin!"

Can you see how effectively this works? All she needs to overcome a sense of not being okay is control her weight, so she can view the right number on her bathroom scale and to be thin enough for people to notice and say something complimentary. The problem is that thinness becomes the primary focus of her life, the only thing she can perceive as important.

Did you notice that her emphasis on thinness and control was to overcome rule #1 of "I'm not so hot?" All that effort and turmoil, just to battle one horribly false assumption! Sadly, the wind affects us all. Our lives take various directions attempting to make up for supposed deficiencies or to reach some unnecessary goal. (Many of our inadequacies are responses to parental and other adult expectations, or what we think they said and wanted.)

Once we understand that we are driven by rules created by the Diabolical Duo, everything we do can come under our control. The idea is to stop doing dumb things because of dumb rules and start doing smart things because of smart rules. Don't let your roots and the wind stop you from living a life that is the right one for you.

WHO CAN YOU TRUST?

Your roots and the wind have given you a sense of identity, a working model of the world and your place in it. For better it keeps things consistent, reduces the amount of information you need to analyze, and helps make sense of what happens in the world. For worse, you give up control and float along with the wind.

Since we looked at Mary Ann's stereotypical woman's vortex of worry, "Does this make me look fat?" it is only fair to gaze upon an equally useless concern from the stereotypical male side. Harry's most recent step away from personal wisdom, courtesy of his version of the wind, occurred last week.

He was looking in the mirror after his Saturday morning shower. "Oh God," he said out loud. He realized at that moment, age 47, (after fifteen years of pretending he wasn't), that he was bald. Half a minute after that realization, he realized his comb-over had been a failure for at least ten of those years, fooling only himself. His shoulders sagged. Then he noticed his paunch. Harry let out a sigh, and the wind continued to blow. Harry's new thoughts now included, "I'll never make senior vice president. I'll never remarry. I'm over the hill. I may as well give up and move back in with my parents." All because of the wind.

Often, I must admit, when a TV commercial comes on for a juicy hamburger, I'm the first viewer rushing out to buy one. Like one of Pavlov's dogs, my mouth waters at the sight of a double-decker with cheese and bacon, lettuce and a couple of pickles.

Think for a moment how you are influenced by television, radio, newspaper, and magazine advertisements. It should be scary how pervasive these manipulations have become in our daily lives. Advertisers don't tell us much about the product; they tell how good we'll feel using it, how popular we will be, how beautiful we will become.

Billions of dollars are craftily spent every year to convince us we are not okay unless we buy and use certain products. Our clothes are not white enough. Our computers are too slow. The food we eat is too fat, not flavorful enough, unhealthy, or not available quickly enough. You name it and we're doing it wrong unless we buy something new and improved.

Today, the wind blasts at us from every direction. Information has become as much a part of us as breathing.

The Internet overloads our circuits; social media is a hurricane of wind. Smartphones are constant companions and bring the world to us. And we become less with every contact.

The only way to overcome your roots and the wind is to have alternatives by which to choose. If you can define guidelines you can trust, that you believe in no matter what, and that you know are right for you, you can overcome these two culprits and live a wise and successful life.

You may wonder how much to trust of what I have presented so far with more to come. After all, my point of view, just like everyone's, is part of the ceaseless wind. The answer is I'm not proposing you do anything. You don't have to change your point of view, modernize your values, or improve your behavior. You don't have to reject religion, quit your job, or disown your family. My message is simple.

The key to separating yourself from the herd is having the perspective to see the truth. Perspective is using your values to evaluate what you see. You must be able to view your life as it is and have the ability to define it just for you. I will suggest and prod, doing my best to shine a light into the shadows of your life. However, your values and your decisions are your own.

The upside is a better life. The downside is more personal responsibility to figure out how to do it. You get what you pay for. There is an upfront cost for claiming your life. I'm suggesting that you think about yourself and what your life is about, pay attention as you go through it, define and monitor what is important, and make sure you do the best you can moment to moment.

Another metaphor to help you understand and cope with roots and the wind is to think of them as part of a bus trip. Roots are someone else driving, someone else choosing the route, someone else making the schedule. The wind is someone walking up and down the bus aisle offering holiday brochures, candy, travel suggestions, and other enticements. It all looks and sounds good. Is it the right bus and the right trip for you?

Q and A

Bob, there were a lot of complicated ideas. Can you summarize in a few lines?

The idea is you must accept, modify, or reject your society's rules to live a life that truly suits you. I was drafted during the Vietnam War. I was opposed to all wars, yet I felt an obligation to my country. I could have shown up for the army, rejected it by moving to Canada, or done something in between. I did not want to kill anyone but wanted to serve my country. To be true to my values, I joined the Navy and continued my objector activities.

What's the relationship between independence and perspective?

It's a cycle. You must acquire a degree of personal wisdom before you can be independent. Teenagers fight for independence, with little personal wisdom. Independence is not blind opposition. Without wisdom, mistakes are made. You have minimal personal wisdom, make independent decisions, learn from that, add to your perspective, make better independent decisions, and so on. With personal wisdom, you will make mature decisions of what to accept about your roots and what not to, and also how to resist the forces of the wind. It's a cycle of growth.

That reminds me, the terms "roots" and "wind" are interesting words. Why did you pick them?

To label them so you can sense them better and to emphasize how strong the effort must be to gain independence. Since these forces form our environment and are thus invisible, I had to make them real and worrisome.

What should I take away from this section?

That from now on, you should know the external forces you automatically accept. Many of them are good, like highway speed limit signs. Some, like "The only good Indian is a dead Indian," are obviously destructive. The ones in the middle require value judgments. Be on the alert for the Diabolical Duo, identify your values and be aware of your moments.

I mean, what should I do differently?

Before you do anything important, ask yourself if this is what you want to do. When you're talking with friends, question what the group may assume to be true—and ask yourself if it really is. When you encounter an idea in opposition to yours, try to understand the underlying assumptions of the other point of view, and see if they are any more valid than your own.

LIFE SKILLS II

Perspective

.

You +

A person starts to live when he can live outside himself.
Albert Einstein

Birds gotta fly, fish gotta swim, humans gotta… what? We humans must learn to see outside ourselves to create a unique life. Independence gives us the opportunity; perspective helps us to do something with the opportunity, most importantly, to create meaning.

I played competitive amateur golf in my early thirties. It was nothing big time, just county and state tournaments with little success. But I practiced a lot and played at a high level. When I played with my dad and his friends, all retirees, they marveled at my long tee shots, how I could curve a shot around a tree, and blast out of a sand trap and end up near the hole. I, with high expectations, would moan and groan if a shot was too far or not far enough. Tee shots, which flew fifty yards past the old guys, would elicit complaints from me if they were crooked enough to end up on the wrong side of the fairway.

On the way home after play one afternoon, my father asked me to stop complaining after a bad shot. "For us," he told me, "your shots are wonderful. We can't do what you do and never will. We wish we could hit just one of what you call a bad shot. It's demeaning and takes away some of our enjoyment of the game when you complain after hitting the ball better than any of us could." He had a valid point.

It was yet another lesson that the way I see a situation is not how anyone else sees it. Was I right to have high goals? Yes. Was my dad right in suggesting I take his friends' feelings into account? Absolutely. That's where perspective comes in. I had to redefine the situation and myself. I was not a competitive golfer when out with my dad and his pals. That game was golf for enjoyment, not winning, not scoring, not hitting perfect shots.

Perspective is not just seeing, it means being able to understand the relationships between life elements and being able to redefine what is important as the relationships between elements change. I had to honor my need to do my best while accepting the unwritten rules of a social game among friends.

Personal wisdom enables you to see yourself separate from the world. Perspective will enable you to understand the relative value of what you see.

You've heard the idea, "The only constant is change." I believe that is true and it should be true with people. It should be but isn't. One assumption of this book is that we don't initiate change as much as we should. Life is movement. Life is change. A predictable life would be boring. Don't fear the unknown, because that's what life is.

Should you redefine yourself? Should you redefine your

roots? Yes, to both. But, don't redefine all the time. Use your perspective to understand what is important, how things work, and how things relate. Assuming things don't change, including you, is idiotic. Everything changes. You must keep up. Personal Wisdom helps you deal with change and gets you where you want to go easier and faster.

As you know, everything has a cost, but so few things have lasting value. What has value today may be worthless tomorrow. Your needs, wants, and wishes make up a catalog with prices listed by how much time it will take, how much money it will cost, and how much emotional investment is at stake. How do you choose between your kid's baseball game and working late for that chance of promotion? What has worth to you? How do you fit into the world? And when do you live as a unique human being?

Others

> *It is not good enough to have a good mind; the main thing is to use it well.*
> Rene Descartes

In eighth grade, one of my classmates, Mary, was the most beautiful woman I knew. And I call her a beautiful woman because she was not a girl like so many other females in my class. Mary had hips and curves moving every which way. Her eyes were deep pools filled with mystery. When she smiled, it wasn't so much friendly as it was promising—of what I had little clue. She was the total woman to this boy who hadn't yet put razor to cheek.

I would gaze at her in class and forget about the teacher, follow her down the hall and trip over my own feet. I would watch her dance with other boys and wish I were bold enough to ask her to dance myself. In gym class, I danced with her once but was so numb with nervousness I couldn't keep to the rhythm, smile, or even talk, let alone breathe.

We attended the same college for a while, gradually developing other friends. She dated someone I didn't know. Within a few years, she had married and moved away.

Twenty-five years later, I saw her again at our high school reunion. She was still total woman. I was older and wiser, certainly more comfortable with myself. I told her of my high school crush. She smiled that smile that was so beguiling and said, (you knew this was coming), "That's too bad, Bob. I wish you had said something. I liked you too."

Had I only known how to approach her. But I didn't have the wisdom. I didn't have the perspective. I didn't have the skills. Your life is made up of what you think, feel, decide, and then do.

Personal wisdom is doing the right things well. So much of our formal education is focused on facts and theories that have nothing to do with being a good neighbor or telling bad news to someone you love. We learn about what it is to be human on the street, in dark places, watching TV, and by trial and often error. Having a few life skills in our back pocket can make a lot of difference. Wouldn't it be great to do things well and learn to do things better every day? The following sections are skills for you to try out as you continue to become independent and improve your perspective.

Caring for Others

Don't ever take a fence down until you know why it was put up.
Robert Frost

Others are the source of the wind. None see the world the same way you do. Everyone wants it their way just as much as you want it your way. The Seven Billion Rule tells you that your opinion is the most valid but shares first place with a bunch of other people, all of them different.

Without other people, life wouldn't be worth living. But with other people, life becomes more difficult. Say I hit you as hard as I could on the arm, and you developed a big, sore bruise. Who is responsible for that bruise? Me, because I hit you? Or you, because it was your body that formed the bruise? If I do something to you, should I be responsible for your reaction? Let's look at it another way. Suppose I said something to you that hurt your feelings. They're your feelings. Should I be responsible if you become upset? Would it make a difference if I knew beforehand you were sensitive about what I would say? How much responsibility does the talker have for what she says, and how much does the listener have for her interpretation and response? Bruises or feelings, we live in a world of individuals constantly bumping against one another.

Take, for example, the victim of a practical joke. The poor victim is sitting with a plateful of noodles on her head, painfully embarrassed, while others look, laugh, and point. If she becomes angry, she gets blamed. "Can't you take a joke?" one of them asks, handing the victim responsibility for the situation.

Every contact between people involves different (and sometimes opposing) assumptions. An important element in living your ideal life is being clear about expectations and responsibilities when relating to others.

RELATING

I'm assuming you are reading this section after taking a break from finishing the last one. If you didn't take time off, what's your hurry? What rule are you following that pushes you to go on so quickly? On the other hand, if you have followed all my suggestions so far, are you a compulsive rule follower? Do you always do what other people ask? A joke that has gone the rounds in psychiatry for decades has it that if psychotherapy patients are early, they're anxious; on time, compulsive; and late, hostile. We're judged no matter what we do.

You may remember that social rules enable the group to survive and the individual to fit in if he or she so chooses. This means that the individual, you, must decide how much of yourself to give up to fit into the group.

A heartache for me as a professional was hearing the

story of wives in their fifties and sixties, and the descriptions of poor marriages they struggled for decades to make better. These women made a commitment for better or worse and got the worse. Maybe even more distressing were those women whose husbands had left them for a bit of arm candy. They have little hope of finding another companion. Each of these lonely, depressed ladies had a similar rule.

"If I do my best, I can make this marriage work and it will last forever."

At first glance, this seems like a good rule because it fits into another one we all know about.

"In order for a relationship to succeed, it needs to be worked on."

Any marriage counselor would tell you something like that. Knowing this, all these ladies worked on their marriages, expecting their efforts would pay off in a good, strong relationship. As time went on, they worked more and more, harder and harder, until the wife realized that she married a jerk or, equally likely, the jerk left.

Sally married this nice fellow named Tom when she was twenty-two and he, at twenty-four, had just begun graduate school. "This is a 50-50 partnership," they decided (but she dropped out of school to support them). Oh sure, they talked about her going back to school, but that would have to wait. He was two years ahead of her and that much closer to a career.

As a man, too, this seemed like a good decision because his work would bring in more money to support a future family. Ah, a future family. A bouncing baby boy, Jeff, arrived just before Tom finished his training. Cute little Nancy came three years after that. Sally worked part-time and ran the household too. It was lucky that a good child daycare center was nearby. So, Sally spent more time at home now and understood Tom's need to work late to get ahead in business.

Because it "had to be this way," maybe the work and responsibility of the marriage and family became 60-40. Over the years, Sally understood Tom's need to relax on the golf course with his buddies every Sunday afternoon. She also understood and forgave his one mistake with the girl across from his office. Over time, Sally's work on the marriage, her emotional investment, became greater and greater.

Tom's focus, meanwhile, became more and more outside the home. Work held his interest and his attention. Home was a place to relax, kick back and avoid problems. He was withdrawing into his own world. Sally sensed that the marriage wasn't as good as it used to be or as she wanted it to be. She redoubled her efforts. She suggested counseling. "But why?" Tom would ask. "I feel OK. Maybe you should see someone if you aren't happy."

A few weeks before Sally saw me for help, Tom had left, taking his now 5% investment in the marriage elsewhere. What did he have to lose? Sally's rule about working on the relationship was a large part of why the marriage failed. If you constantly do more than your share you no longer have a relationship, you have a burden.

My friend, psychologist Dr. Bob Rich of Australia, talks about balance. He says that if one does too much, the other will automatically do less.

There is another common rule many of my clients had that drove me crazy. Again, it is a rule that seems to be a good one that will work for everyone's benefit.

"A good person is nice to others."

It sounds like a rule caring people will abide by, a form of the golden rule. Where it gets people in trouble is trying to be nice when you aren't sure what the other wants, make assumptions, suffer the anxiety of wondering if you're right, and then put too much importance in the other being pleased with what you did.

A good friend of mine was traveling back to Ann Arbor, home of my alma mater, the University of Michigan. In an attack of nostalgia, I asked him to pick up a shirt for me with "MICHIGAN" stenciled across the front. I made it clear I wanted a simple gray T-shirt, the kind I remembered wearing during my student days.

He returned with an up-to-date multi-colored exotic number with buttons, 3/4-length sleeves, and a nifty shaped collar, thinking he had improved on my expectations. All he did was make some assumptions, following his version of the rule of wanting to be nice to me. He was being kind, but I didn't get the shirt I wanted.

He related to me from his own perspective, which is only part of the equation for caring for others.

RULES FOR CONNECTING

Caring for others requires that you accommodate two perspectives, yours and the others'. This is easier with friends since most friendships exist because of similar likes and dislikes. It is more difficult with neighbors and co-workers because other factors have brought you together.

Let's look at your rules regarding others. Your rules for interpersonal relationships must include:

1. Something that defines your role and behavior
2. Some sort of outcome or definition of your expectations

and/or

3. Something defining the other person's role

Here two examples for me:

"I should be funny when first meeting people, so they will like me."

"People like to talk about themselves, so I will encourage them to do so."

With people I know well, I don't need to be funny, I can be myself. Your rules do not apply the same to everyone. You have rules to control rules. Many rules operate only under certain circumstances or are secondary to more important rules.

To relate well to others, you will need to know what rules take control when. For some people, emotional rules take precedence over logical rules when a loved one is involved. Rules may change for different races, religions, ages, situations, etc. For example, a hard-driving businessperson might operate during the workday from a rule of "get the most you can and give away nothing," while at home be a pushover to spouse and children.

Your rules for relating to your spouse, children or close friends will differ from those for strangers. That's only logical. But why is that? You may find it's not that easy to explain. Some people risk their lives to pull strangers out of a burning car without regard for what their own death may cause their family.

You may treat some casual friends the same way you do loved ones only because you see them every day and want to avoid problems. That is a good reason but may not be a good rule to follow. It isn't a good reason if the avoidance behavior is based on a rule like, "I will avoid rather than confront problems with others." This rule is often based on a more general rule like, "Security is more important than resolving a conflict." Can you see how this prohibits connecting?

There are many natural barriers between people. As you have seen, the many elements of your roots and the wind drive us to be someone we are not, do things that are often not in our best interest, and otherwise make it difficult to relate to one another.

Perhaps the greatest barrier is the basic difference of gender. The next section takes a simple, stereotypical look at men and women, stretching gender rules so they are clear and definite, and so you can identify with one or the other, or something in between. See how they apply to you whether you're a lady, a man's man, gay, bisexual, confused, nonbinary, ambivalent, or just curious. We're all in the mix somewhere.

*   *   *

For practice, think of someone you know well such as your spouse or a long-term intimate friend. Do not pick one of your parents. (It is sad how little we learn about them when we could have.) Think of what rules apply to your relationship with that person.

Think of someone else now, a person you like but with whom you are not close; a co-worker, perhaps. What rules guide you to treat this person differently than someone close?

Observe others interacting and try to guess what rules are guiding their interaction. People interactions are not random and the more you know, the better yours will be.

Men and Women

Why can't women be more like men? Most likely, it's due to biological rules. The predilection to nurture, to care-take, to nest, to seek the safety of the group may drive a lot of female behavior and expectations, even those of the highly evolved human female.

Why do men have to be such blockheads? Ah, the effect of man's primordial urges. From the strutting peacock, to an elk's harem, to the gorilla potentate being groomed by his favorite female, the human male psyche has a thousand vestiges in the animal world.

The most unappealing of men can swagger into a group of women expecting them to swoon at his feet. "Hey," he believes with every testosterone-soaked neuron, "I'm an

Alpha Male and they all want me."

The perils of biology are significant. Many of our drives have not caught up with the socialization process, much the same as our morality cannot keep up with technology. Rape, war, robbery, and driving drunk are all uncivilized, but we do these things and more. Personal wisdom is recognizing our natural tendencies and taking responsibility for them.

MEN

Relationships between lovers are one of the most powerful experiences we can have, for good and for bad. Bitter divorces spawn murders, of estranged spouses and sometimes the children. Intense feelings are the norm in intimate relationships. Years before he died, the wife of volatile Ohio State football coach Woody Hayes was asked if she ever contemplated leaving him for a more peaceful life. "Divorce?" she replied, "Never. Murder? Yes!"

More than half a century ago, E. B. White and James Thurber collaborated on a book called *Is Sex Necessary?* a tongue-in-cheek examination of whether two sexes has turned out to be of any benefit to our species. Their conclusion was, although fraught with complexities, the two sexes option was as good as anything else. In this section, we examine gender complexities. Here are a few assumptions we can make to understand this whole business of the opposite sex.

Assumption #1: Men are more goal-oriented than women.

Remember the cliché about a couple making a long-distance drive? The woman sitting in the passenger seat asks the male driver, "Could we stop soon? I need to go to the bathroom." The man replies, "Hold on just another hour. I hate to stop. We're making such great time and we can be there by six." She'd hold on.

Why would a mature, sane woman fidget, rock back and forth, and hold her breath for "another hour?" Why would the man even ask her to "hold on" when stopping would only take a few minutes and be much more comfortable for everyone? (And why is he the one driving anyway?) These gender rules are the work of your roots and the wind. Let's analyze this little verbal exchange and sort out why this happens.

Men (being generally more goal-oriented than women whether driving a nail or driving to Cincinnati) focus on the outcome, the result of their efforts. "Getting there by six" is more important than his (or her) personal comfort.

Would you agree that the man's focus on outcome should allow him to ignore his companion's needs? No? Good, because there is more to this attitude. Men are insensitive for a lot of reasons.

Assumption 1 suggests that men have some rule that mandates placing maximum worth on the goal. Assumption 2 goes more out on a limb.

Assumption 2: Men are less able to sense or pay attention to their emotions and put emotions after other important things like schedules.

Below are more assumptions that your personal experience may validate. It doesn't matter if they are part of your roots, the wind or some combination.

Assumption 3: Men are less able to identify their feelings.

Assumption 4: Men are less able to express their feelings.

Assumption 5: Men need to feel capable.

Assumption 6: Men hate feeling incompetent or uncertain.

Combining these leads to a final assumption about men.

Assumption 7: Men will avoid dealing with feelings because of uncertainty about emotions and the need to be in control and will minimize feelings in others.

Picture a small park in a typical Midwestern town on a warm summer evening. The grass is deep green. A gentle breeze rustles through a grove of elms nearby. In the middle of the park, near a winding brick walkway, a woman is sitting on a bench. She is crying. A man who knows her sees this and walks over to help. He offers his handkerchief and tells her, "Now don't cry, things will be all right." He will feel satisfied if he gets her to stop crying and even better if she nods her head and says she is okay now.

A woman friend happening on this same scene would most likely try to find out what was wrong, sympathize with the woman, and may even end up crying herself. We will investigate this dynamic a little later. Accept that a man approaching this situation would be goal-oriented to the point of wanting the woman to stop crying and be interested in little else.

Emotional reasons for doing something are low on the list of male priorities. Discomfort, someone else needing a bathroom, does not distract a man from his original goal.

The man in the car getting somewhere by six is not only goal-oriented and insensitive but also bossy. There is increasing documentation in scientific and popular literature regarding this social difference between men and women. From this material and the Alpha Male drives, we can make another assumption.

Assumption 8: Men set up pecking orders.

Men tend to be competitive, exposing strengths and weaknesses to sort out who is top dog and who isn't. Men drive the cars, make the decisions, and are captains of the ships.

This is the reason men don't ask directions when lost. What man worth his symbolic-rule-macho-pecking-order-mind wants some dumb, male, pimply-faced, high school dropout service-station attendant knowing more about where he is than he does? "Oh sure," the kid says to the vice-president of finance sitting in his new Lincoln, "I know where that's at. That's easy to find." What is worse than admitting ignorance to the ignoramus would be the vice-president missing a turn or two following the directions and remaining lost, or worse, driving by the station once or twice again, each time making eye contact with the amused station attendant. Few men are man enough to cope with that.

Men want to be the boss (or "let" someone else be boss). Men say things like "Why don't you hold it for one more hour?" Note that, many times, men ask a woman to do such a thing but not another man. You would think the pecking order rule would prompt this behavior between men even more than with women. The reason this is not always done is the fellow at the top of the current pecking order doesn't want anyone riled up enough to challenge his position. In this situation, men will hassle and make fun of one another (which is pecking order banter) before pulling over to let the guy out for a pit stop and keep making fun of him until he gets angry and is about to challenge the pecking order itself.

Let's inspect a typical guy's rules.

Behavior: Getting there by six.

Rule: Reaching a goal means success as measured by driving the route a half-hour faster than George from next door. This means bragging rights for a year.

Behavior: Saying "Hold on..."

Rule: Pecking orders exist; be at the top of yours. Thus, he interprets her "I have to go to the bathroom," as an unimportant request from a subordinate because women (since they emphasize emotions) over-dramatize things.

It gets worse.

Behavior: Telling the woman to "Hold on just another hour."

Rule: I'm the boss so we'll do what I want; and, if she must go, she'll create a fuss.

I expect you women readers will be nodding your heads in agreement. We men do act this way sometimes. But you ladies seem to have rules that encourage our boorish behavior. Can you imagine a woman telling a man to "Hold on a couple of more hours?" He'd get angry, pee out the window, grab the steering wheel, or otherwise make his desires known and many women would pull over. Women tend to give in. So, let's assume things about women.

WOMEN

Assumption: Women are more interested in how comfortably things get done.

This means that women would like problems and issues resolved in good ways, in harmony, with everybody happy. Other people's desires are considered in how problems are approached. The outcome is important but so is the process. Mothers know, for example, of the sacrifices needed to keep everyone in the family happy. They are responsible for chores getting done and family needs getting met.

Women, as a group, act the same way in social situations. Often, when women encounter a swaggering male making dumb suggestive comments, they laugh it off or placate him until he goes away. He leaves with his fantasy identity intact, maybe even reinforced by the women's reactions. They are left feeling intimidated, ashamed, irritated, let down, and resentful.

For the poor woman who had to go to the bathroom but didn't, these rules controlled her responses:

- A good wife supports her husband no matter what.
- If your husband feels strongly about something, give in.
- Make your man happy even if it bothers you.
- Keep the peace.
- Be responsible for others.
- Smile through obnoxious behavior.
- Be a good sport.

The woman in the car subordinates her needs for the common (his) good because she wants to avoid an unpleasant situation.

PUTTING IT TOGETHER

I generalized how men and women operate, simplifying a few gender rules to make the point they exist, not that they are good or bad or always one way. Also, men and women can have similar rules sometimes and different rules other times. These are the kinds of rules, for men and for women, which minimize intimacy. Keep in mind that such rules drive attitudes and behavior and don't let them get in the way. For men and women, gender rules create unnecessary barriers and that makes relating to one another more difficult than it needs to be.

*　　*　　*

Ponder your gender rules. Do you need to have them? Which ones might discriminate? Have they changed as you've matured? Create a few new ones and try them out.

What Women Want

*For most of history,
Anonymous was a
woman.*
Virginia Woolf

Historically, women have had different rights than men. Some would say fewer rights and unequal ones. In Roman times marriage was most often a political or economic arrangement. Women had little to say but a lot to lose. A widow, for example, would lose rights to her husband's property if she remarried after his death. During the Middle Ages in England, an adulteress could lose her nose and ears if caught. For eons, women have been property. Again, in medieval England, if a man carried off a freeman's wife, he was expected to procure the injured party a replacement wife. Even dress was confined by law. A woman was required to dress according to her husband's or father's position. Wives and daughters of servants could not wear veils valued over twelve pence while wives of knights could wear fur only if their husbands had rental incomes at a certain level.

Scottish brides were permitted only two changes of clothes on their wedding day. And such ideas of control were worldwide. In India, the principle was, "Day and night must women be held by their protectors in a state of dependence." Women have been treated as objects, and only sometimes as treasured objects, for thousands of years.

These different rights are derived from holy books, legal distinctions, traditional roles and by how individuals act on these ten-thousand-year-old roots.

Should women have equal rights? Should anyone not have equal rights? Are there any valid reasons for double standards? This book is about individuals fulfilling their potential. Until ancient and not so ancient institutions figure things out, we should attempt to learn what is on most women's minds.

As we noted, women have had a long fight to enjoy even modest rights in society. Much of the fight has been to gain simple equality. The path has been difficult. Women and girls encounter sexual harassment, catcalls, out-right molestation as a daily threat and too often as a terrifying reality.

At the same time, women go out of their way to be attractive. It is a rare woman who just gets dressed in the morning. Most spend a lot of time choosing an appropriate costume. A woman doesn't have the comfort of wearing clothes. She must somehow create an outfit that says the right things in just the right way. That's a lot of work for little return.

Aretha Franklin sang that women want just a little bit of R-E-S-P-E-C-T. That's certainly true, but there is much more. Women have been so trapped by men's biology and the constraints of society it is hard to feel accepted, let alone living as a free and independent human being.

What do women want? Freud couldn't grasp this one. He wasn't even close. Most men don't get it. Even some women can't quite get a handle on what this is about.

Women are driven to make things good for others while swirling in a cauldron of intense competition with one another. The fair sex knows how to improve another's well-being by offering a cup of coffee, listening to a tale of woe, or finding just the right birthday card. At the same time, however, driven by the demands of the wind, women compare themselves to an ideal and to each other. Every mirror becomes a battleground, every change in fashion another mountain to climb. To make matters worse, women don't seem to derive the same reward from achievements as men. The result of all this is a simple one, but of the worst kind imaginable: women need an external measure of worth.

Women give, and give, and give, and give. They worry about everything and everyone all the time. Women need something back. What a relief to be one's self and have someone care.

Not all women need and want the same thing or in the same degree. But, many women, driven by their roots and the wind, want something so simple that they should enjoy it no matter how generalized or stereotypical it might be. It is a gift we can give to help them balance all the stresses they encounter.

What do women want?

Women want to feel special.

This desire to feel special isn't asking a lot, but it is important.

All it takes is a little time, a little effort, a little thought. For men, the return on this investment is ten to one, a thousand to one.

Feeling special happens when another person does something that says, "I took time from my life for you because you are special to me."

"A rose is a rose is a rose?" Not to a woman. Any gesture from one person to another that makes someone feel special is a kindness of the best sort. Women know this, that's why they make it happen for others. Make it happen for the women in your life.

Feeling special is uplifting, women know it and women want it. However, when women gain the RESPECT (self and otherwise) they deserve, feeling special will not be so important.

To gain personal wisdom women must give up the focus on feeling special.

When some women reach their forties, they give up trying to be young and attractive and learn to enjoy being themselves. They stop wearing heels and buy sensible shoes and comfortable underwear. For some of these women, this is giving up, for others it is an opportunity to discover they have been special all along. To live a full and happy life, you must do this earlier if you can and better if you can. Style can be an interest, but no longer a need.

You already know this, but it bears repeating. As far as men are concerned, you're already special. The human male is similar to males of just about every species; they want any available female. You're special as female to men if you're *any one* of these: between 15 and 80 years of age, weigh between 75 and 300 pounds, have breasts and/or hips, use makeup, don't use makeup, have long hair, laugh at men's jokes, enjoy sex, can cook, have large breasts, can throw a ball, like camping, enjoy a beer, are a bit of a mystery, can fix things around the house, and/or smell pretty. It isn't hard to be yourself and be special to men. The above list probably includes 99.999 percent of all the women in the world, so you are covered. Being special to most men is easy. The hard part is to have men consider you as a unique and valuable person, not only an object for mating.

As for your women competitors, learn that you will never win the competition against them. Someone will always have nicer hair, have clothes that fit better, can more easily attract men, be slimmer and fitter, be more attractive, have nicer breasts, smaller waist, longer legs, smarter, friendlier, smaller pores, fewer insecurities, and better chances at everything. Switch from the female glass is half-empty mentality to the masculine the glass is always nearly full. Identify your assets and enjoy whatever they are. Look in a mirror and pay attention to what you like. Enjoy the view of you.

The goal is for you to be unique, to act in the way you truly are, to be comfortable being yourself, and to enjoy being yourself. This can't happen if you stick with wanting to feel special. Feeling special requires someone else to make you feel good about yourself and that can't happen often enough or well enough.

If you need someone else in the equation to feel good about yourself, you will never escape the prison of feeling inadequate. You will always need the fix of that other person's approval.

*   *   *

Many psychological studies support the idea that if you act a certain way, like happy, you'll tend to feel that way. What way can you act that will allow you to enjoy being yourself, so you don't have to chase feeling special? What can you do that makes you glad that you're you rather than someone else? What do you bring to the world every day that no one else does?

You must let go of wanting to be special and learn to be you. This will be scary. You, all by yourself have never been enough. You have needed the right dress, the right hair, the right companion, the right whatever. And you needed the right reaction from the right person, who has always been the wrong person because it hasn't been you.

Seeking this special-ness has been a lifelong effort and you cannot give it up overnight. From learning to put on makeup to forgiving your boyfriend's wandering eye, you have spent a lifetime externalizing your value. A good way of getting rid of this drive is to give it up for a few hours at a time. Learn how to enjoy being you rather than being special.

Instead of making yourself feel special with a bubble bath, candles and a glass of red wine, *enjoy* yourself with a bubble bath, candles and a glass of red wine. Can you see the difference? Pampering yourself is that artificial way of trying to make you feel special. Enjoying yourself is doing what you want to do.

This can be a critical part of your journey toward personal wisdom. Be you first and a woman second; not the other way around as you have been until now.

Regarding men, they are simple creatures, driven by strong biological urges. Men are on the lookout for the next mating opportunity even if they aren't thinking about it or even wanting one. This drive seems to exist for most of a man's life. A man's eyes dart to a female form, ears perk up at the click of high heels. Once a woman is spotted, there is a physical sense of "Hey, there's one." There is a feeling of accomplishment, almost a relief at adding another sighting to some internal biological list. This response is physical including a semi-conscious appreciation of that female's best attributes. Men like whatever they see. At least one element of every woman's femaleness can be found interesting. Men are not so responsive to emotions and intimacy—these are difficult because men are designed for conquest and dominance.

Don't demand they open up, like splitting open a coconut. That doesn't help much. Ask what they feel and reward what little they express. Tell them how much you appreciate their openness and be patient. Men are barbaric. To become civilized and fit company will take a gentle but firm hand. Do not punish men's idiocy, but lavish rewards on small gains. And demand to be treated as an equal. Do not give up one inch of being treated with respect.

What Men Want

Men get that remote control in their hands, they don't even know what the hell they're not watching. You know we just keep going, "Rerun, that's stupid, go, go, go."
Jerry Seinfeld

In the grand scheme of things, males have been predominant. For most of human history, might makes right. Although a person's social contributions are gaining influence, strength and power still affect most decisions. Vestiges of might-makes-right still affect the current edition of male Homo sapiens.

Men are simple creatures with simple and easily defined wants. Thus, men can gain worth from scoring touchdowns, closing big deals, and driving hot cars.

When a man accomplishes something, it reaffirms that he is somebody. Men believe they are in complete control of their sense of well-being.

Compare the human male to a business. If the company is growing at a reasonable rate, owners are happy. If a man is accomplishing things, he feels happy too. Except, deep in the back of his mind, the male is feeling an uncertainty, "Can I keep it up?" (The symbolism here is telling.)

Men can give up being in control in some ways. That's fun. Live on the edge. Race on the freeway. Drive your boat on the lake faster than anyone else. Free climb a steep cliff. Drink until you pass out.

For many men, danger is a high. For almost all men, taking a chance is fun. Bruises are badges of courage. A little blood, or a lot of blood, is cool. Not all men are tough, but all men want to be tough or at least not a wuss. This is another primary physical driver for men.

What do men want? We can get to that quickly.

Men want to avoid feeling vulnerable.

Denial, avoidance, ridicule, ignoring, attacking, and a host of other responses are the man's way of avoiding feeling vulnerable. Much is lost by these knee-jerk reactions, intimacy yes, and working through challenging emotional issues too. Many men would rather put chains on the car tires in a ten-below blizzard than cope with the white-water of emotions.

Men have an almost insatiable drive to make things happen, get something done or provoke a response, even a negative one. If something is happening, good or bad, controlled by them, all is well.

Sometimes, however, the opposite is also comforting. Lounging on a couch tossing down a few brewskis is cool; nothing is being attempted thus nothing can be lost.

Men are in constant competition with each other to be the most invulnerable.

Many men have lost a lot, a marriage for example by ignoring the request, "just tell me you love me," maybe lost a limb after hearing the dare, "I'll bet you can't _____" (fill in the blank), and even lost a life by ignoring severe chest pains, all to avoid feeling vulnerable.

Men, can you accept that avoiding feeling vulnerable has led you to live only a partial life? By guarding your feelings, you haven't experienced all the joys that come with caring about others and being cared about. You can change and live a richer life. By avoiding being vulnerable, you are not only missing out on important experiences of life, but you are being stupid and living a lie. You *are* vulnerable, that's the reality. You are wrong sometimes. You don't know what to do sometimes. You are unable and weak sometimes. There are stronger, smarter, more masculine men in the world. You are not the top dog. You need to accept that and reclaim the truth of your life.

To the degree you are cursed by this flaw, you do things like:

- Boss people around
- Become argumentative at the drop of a hat
- Drink too much or do drugs
- Make fun of others
- Never admit a mistake
- Take foolish chances
- Always look for and point out flaws in others
- Need to feel superior in everything you do

Your job is not to feel vulnerable. No one wants to feel vulnerable. Being vulnerable is one of the worst experiences a person can have. You must do something maybe harder.

You must become truthful.

Here's your situation. You don't have to be a top dog all the time. In fact, you can admit weaknesses and that's a good thing! You can admit being sad. You can confess that you can't do something. You can even admit to being worried or afraid.

Here's a bonus. You don't have to know everything. You don't have to have the right opinion. In fact, don't express your opinion and instead listen to the opinions of others. You are allowed and encouraged, to let others decide. And, you can allow them to be wrong without commenting just as you are learning to allow yourself to be wrong.

There's more. You don't have to be the boss. Other people can be the leader. You might end up someplace great you never would have thought of. Life doesn't have to be you always right, always on top of things, always telling other people how they should do things. Stop it. The world will be a better place, you'll be a better person and you'll live a fuller more enjoyable life—and the best women will find you irresistible.

When others take the lead and things don't turn out well, you don't have to express your holier-than-thou judgment of the situation, your disappointment, what you would have done differently or anything else. Part of personal wisdom is being silent and letting things be under the control of others.

There is more. You can say things like, "I love you" whenever you feel that without thinking about what might happen. Just express what you feel.

When you get good at it, you'll say things like, "I'm worried" or "I can't believe how lucky I am to have you in my life." You just tell the truth about yourself. There is no pressure to perform!

This will take practice, but you can do it. You don't have to be good at it right away. In fact, if you're not good at it and say you're not good at it, you're doing it right.

Learn you don't have to be the boss of anybody. You don't have to be right or in control.

* * *

For you to achieve personal wisdom as a man you must learn how to sense your true feelings and express them, not the ones created by the fear of being vulnerable (your roots and the wind at work). If you can remember that the truth isn't something grand, it's just the truth, you'll get the hang of it and your life will be twice as good as it was before.

Make the question "This is how I feel; how do you feel?" your favorite. If you can say that, mean it, and appreciate that you've learned something, you've succeeded.

Grow up—be a better person now than you were as a testosterone-driven adolescent.

Regarding women, John Gray, the guy who wrote *Men are from Mars, Women are from Venus* would have been more accurate to say women are from Pluto, they are so out-there complicated. They worry about everything, especially about the feelings of others and will appreciate feeling special even when they have become enlightened. You can help them out by taking responsibility to think of others, but you must do so with the right degree of effort.

If you are a totally reliable man, such as always remembering your anniversary and always getting just the right gift, they may feel you have it too rote and they are being treated as an object. For women to thrive there must be an effort made by the other person. It won't be easy, and it seems unfair.

For example, surprising her with a bouquet from the flower shop that's on the way home is not as special as driving across town through snow to get the promised Chinese takeout.

Women like a little uncertainty, a little adventure, a little badness in their men and they are quick to forgive mistakes, so you don't have to be perfect. Recognize that it is both the effort and the result that is important and do it about ten times more often than you think you need to.

What a woman hates is for the man in her life to be a judgmental, negative, opinionated, know-it-all who then takes her for granted. And many men are just that to their women.

If you observe something and can make a negative comment, no matter how true, don't. The best advice men can have about women is from a woman friend of mine: "Always tell the truth, but don't always be telling it."

You notice she misused a word. So what? Stay quiet. She made a driving error. Stow it. You can disagree all you want, just watch out for being disagreeable. It's almost second nature for men to needle each other. It doesn't work across the sexes.

Bottom line: man up, tell the truth, express your feelings, make the effort.

Intimacy

Anyone can be passionate, but it takes real lovers to be silly.
Rose Franken

Intimacy is the most important benefit of being alive. It also requires more from a person than any other human experience. Unlike many other relationship counselors, I didn't tell people that a relationship requires effort and work. Work isn't what helps intimacy exist. Work is necessary to put a square peg into a round hole. A relationship that requires a lot of work by either party won't (and shouldn't) last long. A good relationship requires diligent, committed, nurturing, volitional, passionate, and honest attention.

Work occurs in a relationship when one or the other person is acting from personal rules rather than relationship rules. The more this happens, the more effort must be made by both people and the less the relationship is the focus.

This may sound like semantics but think of "working" on a relationship like this: If you are sacrificing for your partner, and focus on what you are giving up, you are responding to personal rules and are working on the relationship.

If you are focusing on the benefit to you and your partner by what you do and feel fulfilled by doing these things, you are responding to rules of intimacy and thus paying productive attention to the relationship.

Intimacy occurs when two people are no longer responding to individual life rules but are creating *new joint rules* by listening to one another and expressing their true thoughts and feelings.

These new joint rules become more important than any individual rule and are often more important than the individual's life.

Here is a minor but common example. My wife and I share a bathroom. Her hairdryer is always plugged into one of two outlets near the sink. The cord dangles over the drawer for my shaving stuff, hairbrush, nail-clippers, just about everything I use.

Whenever I need to get in the drawer, I must move aside the cord to her hairdryer. Every morning I move the cord. Every night I move the cord. I could get irritated that the cord is constantly in the way. I could ask her to unplug it and put it somewhere else when she isn't using it. But I don't. Every time I move it, I think of her and am glad she is with me, so big deal if I have to move some of her things sometimes.

A good relationship requires many compromises, but few sacrifices. Too much sacrifice ends up with one much-depleted individual and no real relationship.

RULES FOR INTIMACY

It is not easy to be different and intimate at the same time. Any generalizations one person makes about another will reduce connectedness. Any assumptions and judgments, unconscious or otherwise, lessen the chances for it, too. Differences themselves are not obstacles to intimacy. But often, differences define superiority, goodness, power, or acceptability. This is where the problem begins.

The idea is to determine where differences exist between you and your emotional partners and where they don't and to discover if your rules are creating artificial differences or artificial similarities. For example, do you have different rules for how you should express your emotions compared to how your partner should? If so, why? Or, if not, why not?

Remember the Iceberg Rule? This was the idea you know much less than you think about yourself and other people. The most wonderful way to double your awareness and become connected is to listen to and hear someone different, especially someone of the opposite sex. That is part of intimacy, a willingness to accept another's perspective as equal and a similar willingness to share one's own vision.

Intimacy is a willingness to share one's private self and a desire to understand and cherish the other's private thoughts and feelings.

Intimacy is also the desire and the act of sharing, all the way to becoming vulnerable to hurt and creating a bond that is more important than the self.

Here are some examples:

- A woman who has sex with a man so he will like her is not creating intimacy.
- A man who says, "I love you" to stop a fight with his wife is not creating intimacy.

- A man to his girlfriend, "I don't like it when you drive too fast" may create intimacy.
- People walking hand in hand and feeling it, are.
- Telling a difficult truth to a friend is.

Just any expression of emotion is not intimacy. Being angry is not. Any behavior that attempts to create a better mutual bond is intimacy. Any behavior that reduces isolation is intimacy. For example, wrapping a cold child in a blanket is intimacy. "Giving a damn" is intimacy.

Intimacy combines awareness, emotion, presence and expression. Wouldn't it be something to feel an intimacy with the entire world?

ABUSE

Like indifference is the opposite of love, abuse is the opposite of intimacy. Some relationships spiral downward when one or both individuals treat the other with disdain. Abuse is when one person treats another as an object. The person demonstrates, verbally or physically, "I count, and you don't." For the victim, worthiness is first taken away, and then self-worth disappears.

In many male/female relationships, abuse is the pathological form of men wanting to be in control, not wanting to feel vulnerable, and dismissing women's emotional needs. There is no respect, no feeling special. This is when the woman has compromised, then sacrificed, then is victimized.

The woman has become an object.

The evil of this situation continues when she tries to gain respect from the victimizer. Often the dynamic is she receives heartfelt apologies and the appearance of respect until the next time. Once an abusive relationship begins, the only way for the woman to gain respect is to start by respecting herself, to feel worthiness and then enough worth to leave.

Abuse victims often mistrust their own thoughts and feelings. They become paralyzed, at the mercy and under the control of the abuser.

The victim must find the embrace of a supportive community and regain worthiness step by step until self-worth regrows. Then the healing can take effect.

Balance is important in relationships—talk and listen, give and take, love and be loved. Without balance, one is up the other down. Intimacy should be fun, not a struggle.

BEING SILLY

Rose Franken (1895-1988) was an American writer known for her Claudia stories exploring relationships. Her quote, "… it takes real lovers to be silly," which began this section, makes a good point. When silliness is too frequent, it becomes tedious and a barrier to intimacy. But imagine two people, foreheads together, eyes locked, smiling, giggling. Magic.

*   *   *

Think of your rules regarding intimacy in these categories of rules: social, age group, religion, symbolic (the man should be the initiator), family, and situation (what you like to do, and when you do or don't follow other rules).

- Which of these rules cannot change? What rule says that they cannot and why?
- Which ones can change?
- What's the rule that allows you to change?

- If you were of the opposite sex, what rules would change?
- Why?
- How have your intimacy rules changed as you've gotten older?
- How have they changed as you've gotten wiser?
- What rules do you think are part of your roots or the wind?
- What are you going to do about these old influences?
- What does this all mean?

Take this new awareness about intimacy and figure out areas that make caring for others difficult. Talk to your friends about these ideas, and then bring up other elements of your roots and the wind, such as age differences, regional differences, religious differences, differences in intelligence, race, and character. This is not to eliminate differences. The idea is to maximize appreciation of the differences and eliminate the barriers between you and everyone else.

A common rule that may enhance intimacy is "never go to bed angry with one another." One that may make intimacy more difficult is "Never give in; it is a sign of weakness." It's folk wisdom that bride and groom bring a lot of baggage into a marriage, and this is true, including a host of rules from Mother and Father, the culture, social norms, and whatever else is packed into the emotional suitcase. Lovingly creating new joint rules is the optimal way to build a strong marriage or any intimate relationship.

It isn't you or me or even you *and* me; it's us!

Your Teachers

Would you agree that other people, those who aren't like us, gangsters, liars, cheats, and all the other bad humans, are trying to live a life they consider of value just as we are? A drug addict shooting up in a dark alley is trying to feel good, not any different in intent from an executive enjoying a scotch on the rocks in the evening or a young family taking a bike ride together on a sunny Saturday afternoon.

If so, this means we're all alike and trying to do much the same things, albeit with a wide range of abilities and choices. The difference might only be the skills each has to identify options or make good decisions, available resources, or other hard to control forces.

Sometime around my fifth year in practice, I relearned the lesson that everyone is my teacher. My client was a man on parole from jail. He was put in jail for beating his infant daughter. His parole officer recognized that this man was not a child abuser, but mentally impaired, lacking any semblance of parenting skills. The father did what he thought was right to stop his child from crying. My job was to help him develop the ability to take good care of his little girl, which he was learning.

One day, he asked if his wife could come in and talk to me. When I said sure, he went out to the waiting room and brought back a skinny little woman with buck teeth and scraggly hair pulled back with a cheap ribbon, wearing a faded and threadbare yellow dress three sizes too big. Anyone could tell by her appearance and her speech she was impaired too, probably more than her husband. He presented her to me, told her where to sit and to tell me the problem. Nervously, and with her eyes fixed on the ceiling, she recited from memory what she had obviously practiced the night before.

A few days earlier, she was waiting at the bus stop and three teenage boys arrived. They taunted her, making fun of how she looked. She knew she looked different from other women, that she wasn't like them in so many ways. She told her story in a halting voice as if she were reliving every moment of her humiliation. With the innocent eyes of a child, she looked at me and asked, "Don't they know I have feelings too?" That brought tears to my eyes.

I later wondered how many times I was guilty of something like those insensitive young men. People who are different, who anger us, who are strangers, who for whatever reason don't appeal to us are still people. They are people like you and me. Even our enemies are.

If you think about it, your enemy could be a useful teacher. It's a similar idea to Nietzsche's observation "That

which does not kill me makes me stronger." Your enemy is
going to happily point out errors and weaknesses, give you
no quarter, and never ease up or let you forget. What better
way to improve perspective than to listen to someone who
doesn't appreciate yours? You must be wise enough to listen
and learn, and not absorb the barbs. If you can do this, you'll
have done well.

*   *   *

Your assignment is to learn from a few of your many
teachers. We will begin with close friends and move outward,
so to speak. You can tell these people why you are doing this,
or not. It's up to you.

Tomorrow, talk to your next teacher. Choose a good
friend you can talk to first. A good person to choose is one
with whom you have had intimate discussions before. Ask
this person these kinds of questions (Use other questions if
you wish, but be as specific for yourself as you can):

- What are my best qualities?
- What are the qualities I need to work on?
- What is something I can learn from you about life
  I might not know?
- What is the most important thing about being
  alive?
- What gets you out of bed in the morning?

Then, identify someone who you can talk to who is not a
close friend, but someone you like and who likes you, a
coworker perhaps. Ask the same set of questions.

Next, find someone you don't know well and don't think
you like much. This might be a coworker with whom you
have had scant contact because you both feel that talking with

each other would be irritating, or perhaps a neighbor and both of you seem content to keep a nodding acquaintance. Ask the same questions.

If you're doing well so far, try the ultimate. Find someone who doesn't like you and ask the questions. If you're not comfortable doing this, which is understandable, at least promise yourself that you'll do your best to appreciate the opinions of those you care little about when they express their point of view.

You may find it enlightening to go over the answers you received during this exercise and see if you can interpret what rules the people you talked to were operating from. However, keep in mind the Seven Billion Rule and the Iceberg Rule.

Some of these tasks may be too difficult. If they are, do the next best thing. When someone is critical of you, like a boss, keep in mind they can be your teacher if you let them.

Once you learn that everyone is your teacher (and that's everyone including your kids), you will be expanding your perspective.

Mistakes

Early on we talked about our roots and the wind directing our lives. These forces proclaim we should regret our mistakes. This section declares that you can gain perspective by admitting your mistakes, fixing them as well as you can and moving on.

Mistakes are when you have done something or neglected to do something that results in a bad situation for you or somebody else. Your life can be affected directly, like when you bang your thumb with a hammer, or indirectly, as when you have hurt someone and feel terrible about it.

As far as I know, no one in the history of humankind has ever made a mistake on purpose. Such a thing is impossible. By definition, a mistake is something that went wrong, a bad decision, something changed, not enough information, whatever. If we knew the outcome beforehand, the mistake would not have been made. This section looks at mistakes and problems, and at bad habits, which are mistakes in slow motion.

We are all goal-oriented, and without exception, the goal we seek is something positive. When we make a mistake, it means the goal has not been reached as expected and something bad has occurred instead. It does not matter how flagrant the mistake was, how easily it might have been prevented, or how hurt anyone is. A mistake is an accident and as normal as any human act can be.

I had a client come to me once because he'd killed a man, hitting him while driving five miles an hour in a parking lot. He was tormented by the "if onlies." If only I had seen him, if only he hadn't leaned over to pet that black Lab, if only I hadn't needed cigarettes, if only I had gone left instead of right, and on and on. The lethal sequence of interlocking events was driving him crazy. Had any one thing been different, that young husband and father would still be alive, and my client would not have suffered such overwhelming remorse.

HINDSIGHT

Under most circumstances, making a mistake is nothing to criticize yourself for doing. If you knew more, you would have not made the same decision. But you didn't know more. Even hindsight isn't twenty-twenty.

Take the mistake of arriving at the airport too late to catch a flight. Hindsight would lead you to conclude that trying the new shortcut was a mistake. "Next time," you say to yourself, "I'll know better." But was it the shortcut? What about the soothing music on the clock radio you snoozed through for an extra ten minutes? What about the extra crowded parking lot? What about all the other times you'd left yourself the same time to get to the airport and made it okay? Maybe trusting those earlier experiences was a mistake. The real mistake in making a mistake is missing what could be learned from it. Long-term remorse over a mistake is narrow-minded and shortsighted, a form of self-depreciation none of us can afford. Learning from mistakes and fixing them is perspective.

We sometimes act in ways that can create mistakes because the potential outcome is so positive, we take a chance. I once observed a teenager walking across a hardwood floor holding the base of an empty wineglass between his thumb and index finger. From his sudden smile, you could tell he must have gotten the urge to flip the glass and catch it by the base. The chances were high that an expensive glass would end up shattered into little shards all over the wood floor and he would be in big trouble. His gleeful look before he did it suggested that his desire for joy (by accomplishing the trick, which he did) would overcome his better judgment of carrying the glass safely into the kitchen.

Here the anticipated joy outweighed any negative result. Most problems have the same root. Whatever bad happens won't be all that bad, and the good will be oh-so-very-pleasant. Sometimes, factors cloud our perceptions so that negative consequences don't even exist. Teenager drivers can speed down residential streets because they have no conception that a child could dart out from between parked cars.

Some men can harass women because that's what they believe they're there for. We often run into problems because we don't expect to.

Think of a mistake you had made and what caused it.

Given the circumstances, was there any way to prevent the mistake?

There is a lesson here if we're able to learn it. If we're going to live by personal wisdom, even though we'll make our share of mistakes, then mistakes must be productive. We cannot pretend that an error was not a big deal if it was. We cannot wallow in wishing we didn't do what we did. The lesson is threefold:

- We must work as hard as we can on our choices moment to moment.
- We must rectify our mistakes as well as we can.
- We must learn something, forgive ourselves, and move on and do the same with the mistakes others make.

HABITS

We are compelled to repeat some mistakes because they are part of a chain of behaviors. These mistakes become bad habits because this sequence is stronger than our ability to create a new chain without including the mistake.

Smoking is a good example. Most smokers know smoking is unhealthy. Yet, people continue to smoke for a host of reasons (including physical addiction). Many smokers have a habitual cigarette to relax while driving home from work. For a smoker who smokes to relax, enjoying a smoke after a hard day at work far outweighs the distant threat of dying from cancer. Not smoking would produce tension, a more negative short-term outcome than having the cigarette. In addition, the possibility of that one cigarette causing cancer is so small that it is dismissed.

A bad habit is more positive (enjoyable) than it is negative in the short run, and often the long-term effects aren't part of the decision-making process.

Habits and decisions that may end up as disasters are motivated by the expectation of a positive result. To eliminate bad habits or reduce the number of times you do something stupid, you must sort out the good and bad of your behavior.

Keep in mind that all action rests on the belief it leads to some good. So, if you find yourself burdened with bad habits or often saying to yourself "How could I have been so stupid?" remember that there is good in there somewhere.

For example, some people have the bad habit of interrupting others during informal conversations. This is a bad habit because it is impolite, irritates the speaker, frustrates listeners interested in what the speaker has to say, and sidetracks the discussion. The payoff is the interrupter has the floor and is meeting personal needs.

Once you identify the benefit of the bad habit, your job is to find less harmful, but equally enjoyable ways to enjoy the benefit(s) of the habit. The interrupter could, for example, define his goal as attention and wait expecting others will give full attention later. It's a matter of knowing what you want and finding a better way of getting it.

We must allow ourselves to make mistakes, for that is part of being what we are, but we must not ignore mistakes or try to cover them up like a cat in a litter box.

*   *   *

Beginning today, spend special time in front of the bathroom mirror. While looking at yourself, admit to a mistake each evening. Think of the outcome you wanted and what happened. Separate your worthiness from the mistake. Acknowledge the mistake and your desire to do something about it.

If you can, come up with a new mistake, a way to fix it, and a way to learn from it every day for a week. Practice separating your self-esteem from your mistakes. By doing this, you are weakening the wind and refining your defining moments.

Think about it with these elements:

1. The mistake
2. Desired outcome
3. Actual outcome
4. How are you going to fix it?
5. What have you learned from it?

Coping with mistakes is a powerful way to learn perspective. Personal wisdom is acquired when we learn and change.

Solve Every Problem*

Whether you think that you can, or that you can't, you are usually right.
Henry Ford

Imagine you're driving on a two-lane country road, cruising along listening to music, enjoying yourself, feeling good. On your right is a deep ditch filled with brown water. On your left is a line of cars speeding by you in the opposite direction. About thirty feet in front of you is an old pickup truck piled high with empty steel oil drums tied down with a yellow nylon rope. The load is swaying from side to side. One of the oil drums bounces, slips free and falls upright onto the middle of your lane. What's the first thing you do?

Most people say, "Slam on the brakes!" But, that's not

---

* This idea is more fully described in the book, *The HST Model for Change* (Brown, 2017) as Harnessing the Speed of Thought, a five-step problem-solving process applied to organizational change.

what you do first. Slamming on the brakes, panicking, or any other response is number five of the five responses that occur in this or any other problem.

I am using the example of an impending car crash to show how quickly our 12,000-years-out-of-date brain leaps to a solution. In the example, a quick response is a good thing because it will avoid an accident. But in daily living, this speed becomes a liability. Too often, we rush to solutions without paying enough attention to other making-a-considered-choice-of-what-to-do steps.

Let's go slowly and deliberately through the steps so you can solve a problem or know that it cannot be solved. In the next chapter, we'll slow down this mental process even more.

First, any time there is a change in your environment, like a steel oil drum falling onto your lane, or a new tax law, or the person you hoped to marry telling you it would be better to be just friends, you must accurately define the issue or problem. After the dust settles, make sure the problem is the right one to address.

I used to use the image of a hay bale falling onto the road as my example instead of an oil drum until a trucker told me he'd "drive right through that sucker." He didn't define the situation as a problem. For him, a driver of big rigs, a hay bale in the road was nothing. Similarly, if a box of tissues had fallen from the truck, you would have noticed it, but not defined that as a problem either.

So, first, you must determine if an issue exists and then define what it is.

> *Step 1 Define the issue: There is a steel oil drum in the middle of my lane.*

Once you have decided that a problem exists and is one that requires your attention, you must then decide the result you want. Unless you have defined a goal, your behavior may as well be random. That makes sense, doesn't it? Unless you have some idea of the outcome you seek, you can't know what to do. Or, unless you know where you want to go, you cannot determine the best way of getting there.

Step 2 Define the goal: I want to avoid an accident.

Now we know what we want to accomplish. Often goals are too vague to be of much use, and often, they combine what you want with how you'll get it. Remember; keep separate *whats* and *hows*.

Next, we need to determine things in the way of reaching our goal, those bits of reality or our assumptions that will inhibit or prohibit us from reaching our goal. This stage, when done well, can prevent a lot of grief and wasted time. In our oil drum example, we would consider that cars are whizzing by on our left, that there is a water-filled ditch on the right, and that the estimated time of impact with the oil drum is 1.45 seconds.

Step 3 List hurdles and concerns: Watch out for other cars. The ditch! Quick!

Any solution you choose would need to overcome those factors. Also, if you had more time, your mind would search its memory and recall that the brakes had been acting funny lately and that you meant to have them fixed.

Sometimes our lives are inhibited by imaginary hurdles and concerns, those cast-in-concrete rules of inadequacy, uncertainty, and fear (that you know as the Diabolical Duo). These can be things like our boy and his fear of white dogs or our Lady-of-the-Bathroom-Scale. Often this internal reality is stronger than the external reality. Just because these hurdles are imaginary is no reason to ignore or discount them. Including them will enhance your problem-solving. You can't overcome what you don't acknowledge.

In our impending car crash, some people might sense fear building up, more than they can handle. They become scared and react to fear rather than the oil drum. It takes practice to acknowledge this kind of internal reality and then to ignore it well enough to focus on solving the problem at hand. Athletes and businesspeople have learned to do it, so can you.

In some situations, this point in the five-step process might suggest that the problem, as defined, cannot be solved. For example, if the time to impact was 0.45 seconds, this would be an impossible obstacle to overcome and you could not avoid an accident. Another goal, however, of minimizing injury, could be reached. You would cover your face or fall to the seat. Make sure the goal, as you compare it against all the hurdles, can be reached before you move beyond this step.

After three steps, the goal is well defined, the hurdles or obstacles listed, and the problem is one that can be solved (i.e. the goal can be reached). The next step is creative.

Step 4 List solutions:
- Slam on the brakes
- Swerve to the right
- Swerve to the left
- Panic
- Swear
- Jump out of the car
- Push on the gas pedal
- Scream, etc. etc.

Notice some solutions are silly or dangerous. At this stage

of the process, it doesn't matter. You are trying to create an uncensored list that will give you the maximum options.

The rest is easy.

Step 5: Choose the best solution: Slam on the brakes.

If this works: great. But in real life, the first try doesn't always work.

"Oh, oh." We are skidding into the oil drum. "I should have gotten the stupid brakes fixed!"

On every step, you may have to revise as needed.

Remember that deep ditch on the side of the road? It ended about ten yards back. So, keep pushing on the brakes and now swerve to the right. "Whew." We made it. When we realized that braking wasn't doing the job, we took another look at hurdles and solutions.

We had the same problem; the oil drum was still on the road. Same goal; we still wanted to avoid an accident. But, the obstacle of the ditch on the side of the road, which at first made swerving to the right a bad solution, was gone so we could use swerving as part of the solution too.

This five-step problem-solving process can solve problems or determine if a problem, as defined, can't be solved.

* * *

On the next page are the five steps. Write them down and put them on the refrigerator or on a card for your pocket so you remember to use them all the time.

The Five-Step Problem-Solving Process (also known as Harnessing the Speed of Thought (or HST)

1. *Identify the issue (problem or opportunity)*
2. *Define a goal in measurable terms*
3. *List hurdles and concerns*
4. *List possible solutions*
5. *Choose the best solution*

Resolve Every Conflict

He who knows only his own side of the case, knows little of that.
John Stuart Mill

Conflicts are almost always because the parties involved define the steps of the five-step process differently. The parties are presenting their version of step five, the solution, unaware their steps one, the issue and two, the goal, are different. This is true even if the conflict is about a fact, such as who holds the long-distance underwater swimming record.

When people fight about a documentable fact, some fuel for the argument is symbolic. Maybe the real issue is a need to win or to be dominant or to impress somebody. This is an unstated, undefined, and often unconscious goal. Often, after a smartphone search defines a winner, the loser will defend his position stating, "You didn't understand what I was saying," or do other things to reach his undeclared goal.

Rarely are conflicts simple disagreements. Often, the real issues are never identified.

Take an argument about a curfew between father and son. The son pleads for one a.m. The father says midnight. This conflict will never be resolved because neither is stating all the issues. Part of it is symbolic, some are age rules, others gender, and so on.

Below is a brief summary of this family battleground. The argument is about how late the son can stay out, but the actual elements of each step are left unsaid. For example, the stated issue is to decide on a curfew, but look at all the others.

Step 1 The issue: How late can the son stay out?

For the father, other issues include:
- I need to stay in charge
- I'm anxious when he is out
- I had an earlier time, and it worked for me

For the son, these are other elements:
- I want to feel more adult
- I want to be like the other guys
- I want to impress the girls

Step 2 The goal: One a.m. for the son and midnight for the father

For the father, the goal also includes:
- Make sure the son is safe
- Keep part of his fast depleting authority
- Not give in like the wife always says he does

And for the son:

- Stay out as late as Kevin
- Stay out later than Sharon
- Not feel like a child

Step 3 The hurdles and concerns:

Hurdles for the father:
- I feel like I must win this one
- Already promised the wife I wouldn't give in

And for the son:
- I feel like I must win this one
- Already promised Kevin I would stay out later

If father and son first defined Step One, the issue, as:

"Deciding appropriate curfew" and spent enough time at Step Two to define their mutual goals, this could result in both agreeing that the goal should be measured by:

1. Both satisfied with the decision
2. Safety
3. Comfort with peers
4. Etc. etc.

then the rest is easy, or at least father and son know what they are trying to accomplish will benefit both.

Knowing they are working toward a mutual goal makes a significant difference in satisfying both people's needs and encourages a productive discussion.

Remember the Seven Billion Rule? Every person is unique, and every individual sees things differently. Thus, everyone will define every problem and every goal differently, at least at first.

To prevent you and someone else from falling into conflict, make sure you define the issue and goal together. This is critical because each of you will define the issue and goal differently and rush to present your respective solutions. If you and the other person define a mutual issue to resolve before defining mutual goals, the rest of the work is easier. The difficulty is acknowledging the real issue(s), having the patience to stay on the issue and not jump to a solution, and not sneaking in solutions as part of the issue or goal.

When I lead seminars on this material, I often conclude my presentation by picking out a small group of six or seven people to solve a problem. I give each of them a pretend $20,000 to spend on a week's vacation. There is only one catch. They must spend the vacation with the other people in the group and everyone must agree on where to go. At every seminar, each group immediately presents preferences of where to go. Arguments soon follow: "I don't want to go to France. I'd rather go skiing in Colorado."

Even though I just explained the five steps, these little groups race to step four, presenting individual solutions, often within seconds of my presentation. Since I already defined the problem for them, they should have spent a few minutes defining a mutual goal without declaring how the goal should be reached. For example, some folks define a vacation as a time to get away and relax. Others want adventure. Some enjoy sightseeing. Others want to meet new people and taste new foods. A few want to learn new skills. You can see that unless these differences are sorted out in the beginning, no one will give up their personal, very good solution that reaches their personal, very good definition of an enjoyable vacation. By following the five steps, a mutual definition of a vacation can be found, just as most conflicts can have a mutual goal. If a mutual goal is impossible, then the process is stopped, and a new issue defined, or, both parties accept that the conflict, as defined, cannot be resolved.

*   *   *

Observe how people resolve problems, especially in meetings. See if they rush to step four and have no idea about mutually defining issues and goals.

Go through the steps with a good friend with whom you have a small disagreement. First, define the problem together. Make sure the problem is an issue, not a solution. One clue is if it includes any action, or "should." For example, "Getting everyone to show up at meetings on time," is not a problem. The problem might be boring and unproductive meetings. People showing up on time is a possible goal or even a solution to another problem. Creating productive meetings could be a goal or a solution strategy. A second way of making sure you have defined an issue and not a solution is to go to the next step and define the goal. Take as much time as you need with your friend to make sure you agree to the goal. Then make sure the goal is the correct one for the identified issue.

If you can identify a goal that both of you agree to, you have defined the issue well and defined a good goal if you define the goal in mutually agreed to measurable terms. Decide together how the goal should be measured. For example, if the goal is sharing the use of a lawnmower, you may decide that you have done it well only if you both use it when you want to.

Now both of you list obstacles as you see them. You can take turns, make two lists, or any other way you like, just make sure you both agree all are obstacles and concerns.

When all goes well, your solutions may be similar, but

even if they are not, you can discuss how each one can reach the goal and overcome the obstacles. If one from each list is good, it doesn't matter which one you choose. If it matters, then another problem exists, like you are competing against each other. But take the fifth step, pick one, and try it out. If it works, fine, if not, go through the process until you are both satisfied.

And keep practicing. This is a counter-intuitive process and takes time to learn to do well.

Last, PLEASE, to avoid a conflict growing into an argument, make sure you discuss the initial description of the issue. If someone says, "You hurt my feelings last night." DO NOT say, "Well, last week you hurt my feelings…"

Personal Wisdom and your ideal life depend on realizing your point-of-view is unique. Listen to the other's concerns and respond to them before voicing your own. It works well for everyone. Do not try to win an argument but resolve a conflict. This is how it works: If you think you're right, examine the other person's point of view, anyway. If you may be wrong, so be it. You've been wrong before. An ideal life isn't a sham. You can be living your ideal life and still be wrong sometimes. Learn from it and add to your personal wisdom.

Impossible and Near Impossible Problems

Live dangerously and you live right.
Johann Wolfgang von Goethe

Some problems are lose-lose propositions. It may look like there is a choice, but often there isn't. Hobson's choice problems are like choosing which overdue bill not to pay or deciding to put a parent into a nursing home. These kinds of issues, as defined, don't have a comfortable solution. You're challenged to find the most beneficial solution even though it may be the most distasteful one. It's useful to re-define the problem so that there is a least bad solution or recognize that the problem, as defined, cannot be solved. Some issues have so many solutions that it is difficult to know what to do.

Often what works best in this situation is to take time to list all the pros and cons you can think of for the solution.

You can even have relative values for each measure of the goal, like cost is less important than ease of use. This method often works best when buying something like a car, television, or even a house. For a house, you might say location is most important, a deal-breaker perhaps, then list size of bedrooms, number of bathrooms, square footage, commuting distance, etc. Then you decide by determining which house best meets your important criteria.

Sometimes listing pros and cons makes the process more complicated. What if you made some of your less significant decisions by flipping a coin or putting a list of alternatives on a dartboard and flinging a dart at it from ten feet? Most likely you'd end up with something you wouldn't have chosen using the pros and cons method. This could be a marvelous result.

Say you want to buy a new car and you're a Ford man, or a Toyota lady or even a Caddie granny. Next time you're in the market for a new car, you could list what features you like and list all the makes and models that fit your criteria. If there are only two, you flip a coin and go with that. If there are several possibilities, put the list on the dartboard and fling away. The result will take you away from your normal mode of thinking, maybe break a habit or expand your boundaries.

Try this method next time you're in a restaurant. Open the menu, close your eyes, point, and order. Try the same thing when you plan your next weekend away. Live at least part of your life by chance. Logic is good. Logical things result in a knowing nod of the head. But taking a chance, at least sometimes, brings out the laughter. And you might even learn more by flipping a coin than you would from doing library research.

For example, Annette had been job hunting for months. Now, as often happens, she had to choose between two terrific offers that arrived the same day. It was driving her crazy. She analyzed, she listed pros and cons, she asked her friends and then she called me. I suggested a special coin flip, Dr. B's easy-way-to-make-difficult-decisions. It works like this. If you can't make a difficult decision but you must, find a coin, the bigger the better. Say "heads I'll do X, tails I'll do Y." Then flip the coin. But you don't automatically do what the coin tells you. The secret is to note your emotional reaction when the coin lands. If you feel joy or relief at how it comes out, fine, do whatever it tells you. If you feel bad, if you are thinking "two out of three," then do the opposite of how the coin landed.

And if that doesn't work, which Annette said was the case, we're back to impossible problems.

"Maybe the jobs are equally good, that's why you can't choose," I suggested.

"What?"

"You may be operating from the rule that there always has to be a best way and you have to find it."

"Ah. My roots saying, I must figure out the one-true-best-optimal-choice. And, in this case, there isn't one."

"You got it. Some of us have a rule that says that only the best is acceptable. Rarely is that true, if ever."

"Thanks."

"You're welcome."

Since many of life's problems involve other people, good communication skills are necessary to resolve them. They're easy to acquire once you understand the basic elements. The next section will help you do that.

*   *   *

For a week, try these ways of problem-solving. Then keep doing it for the rest of your life.

Organizing Your Thinking

Language exerts hidden power, like a moon on the tides.
Rita Mae Brown

Those who didn't take a journalism class in school missed a great opportunity to learn an effective way to organize thoughts, which is the first step in being able to communicate them.

Wars have been lost because messages were unclear, and companies have suffered critical losses when business decisions weren't thought out. Clear thinking and good communication are important in human relationships, sharing information, negotiating relationships and making business deals, and in developing perspective.

The basic formula for communicating ideas, making a request, or negotiating actions is journalism's 5 Ws and H. Communication is often best done in this order: Who, What, Where, When, Why and How. Below is a simple phone call from Susan to the maintenance department. Susan and Sid cover all the steps.

> The phone rings *Good morning, maintenance, this is Sid, may I help you?*
>
> **Who**: Good Morning, this is Susan Smith from the 22nd floor. **What**: Our trash is overflowing. Can you come and empty them?
>
> *Sure. Our motto is "You trash it, we clean it."*
>
> **Where**: That's good news. The cans are all over the south end of the floor.
>
> *The south end of the 22nd floor. Got it.*
>
> **When**: Can you do it today?
>
> *We're swamped today. Can you wait until tomorrow?*
>
> **Why**: I'd rather you did it today. Some of it is starting to smell.
>
> **How**: *I can send one person over to get the worst of it in two hours and finish the rest tomorrow. Is that okay?*
>
> Sounds good. Thanks.

In many cases of communicating, one party is the one in need, the receiver (or customer), and the other the provider. Here, Susan is the receiver. Know when you're a receiver and when you are a provider. Exchange information and negotiate how to meet the need.

Whenever you take a message, you are a provider. You are responsible to get all the relevant information. This is where using the five W's and H can ensure an accurate note. Quotes in messages help improve accuracy too.

Effective negotiation requires clearly defined goods or services and a proposal of "I'll give you X if you give me Y." It's useful to keep all the possible Ws and Hs as separate negotiating points. In this way, you can agree on what will be done, then negotiate when. If *when* becomes contentious, you can then go back to *what* and renegotiate it as part of the package of what and when. For example, you agree to buy a car for $20,000. Then you discuss the delivery date. You are told the best they can do is five weeks. You then can say, "Gee, five weeks is too long. I'll tell you what, if you knock $500 off the price, I'll wait the five weeks."

The 5 W's and H are a useful way to keep things organized and get things done. Employees (and children), for example, do best when the objectives are clear and the why is explained. This approach is a great way to make good things happen.

*   *   *

Tomorrow, listen to conversations around you. See how many contain the 5 Ws and H. Notice what is missing. Notice how poorly we communicate and commit to improving how well you do it.

The Ultimate Communication Technique

The true spirit of conversation consists in building on another man's observation, not overturning it.
Edward Bulwer-Lytton

A skinny undergraduate geek, wearing glasses with thick, black frames, was playing a pickup basketball game in a downtown Detroit gym. Most of the players were streetwise toughs, competing in a rough, no blood, no broken bones, no foul game without referees. This student, let's call him Hubert, was, at six feet two, the tallest player on his team. He was also the skinniest. Hubert played center for his team, opposite a hulking brute nicknamed Bruno or Spike, or Killer, something like that.

Killer was six feet six of muscle and mayhem. He also cheated. He made it a practice to camp under the basket where his teammates could toss the ball too high for Hubert to block. Killer caught the ball, pushed Hubert aside, turned, and dropped the ball in the basket. The official rules of basketball called for him to move out of his position at least every three seconds so such a height advantage couldn't be used, but Killer or Spike or whatever his name was didn't care about the rules.

Hubert, however, was a psychology student. He would figure out a way to stop Killer from cheating in the three-second zone and give up some of his size advantage. The first possibility was to demand that Killer stop his cheating. Hubert realized this approach could get him beaten up. He could beg Killer, but that would lead to getting beaten up too. However, by combining ideas he had learned in psychology classes so far, he realized what he had to do.

There are two fundamentals of communication (both to overcome the Seven Billion Rule). One is that you must create a definition of the situation that is mutually satisfactory. The other is that you must always get feedback to make sure you and the other person understand each other.

Hubert kept these two ideas in mind and right there on the court, invented the ultimate communication technique he later called *Ob-Quest*, short for Observation-Question. He realized he had to get Killer to see the situation the same way he did.

The first order of business was to state his observation in positive or at least neutral terms so that Killer wouldn't become angry and punch Hubert's lights out. Then, Hubert reasoned, he had to get Killer to take responsibility for the situation. He could do that by asking the right feedback question.

So, during a lull in the action, Hubert went up to Killer and said, "You know Killer, you're too good a basketball player not to obey the three-second zone." That was a positive observation and a true description of the situation. Then, Hubert asked the coup de grâce question, "Don't you agree?" How could Killer respond? He could say he wasn't good and had to cheat or he could agree with Hubert's observation. Which is what he did, "Yeah, yeah," he replied sullenly. That was the feedback Hubert needed. And Killer started to move out of the three-second zone.

Hubert's question was a bit of manipulation, set up by his observation and by his frustration. The less leading and more positive the observation and question, the more likely it will foster positive communication. By stating your observation, you are declaring the topic from your vantage point. You then need to find out how the other person views your observation and you do that by asking the most relevant question.

I was once in downtown Seattle with five dollars in my pocket. It was way after lunchtime, and I was starving. The aroma of teriyaki pulled me through the open door of a nearby restaurant. Their lunch special was $5.95 and iced tea from a cooler was a dollar. I didn't have enough for the meal, let alone adding a beverage. Using *Ob-Quest*, this happened.

"Wow," I said. "That smells so good. All I have is five dollars and I want to have a little lunch and an iced tea. Is it possible for you to give me three dollars worth of the special and an iced tea?" With a laugh, they heaped up my plate, gave me an iced tea, and motioned to a table near the window. I enjoyed a terrific lunch.

A generic version of *Ob-Quest* is something like, "This is how I see the situation; how do you see it?" And you are off and running with creating a mutual reality and getting feedback. If both parties know this technique, the communication will be smoother than Hubert's pink-hued undergraduate cheeks.

MORE USES

This is also the approach to take when you're using the five-steps to solve every problem or resolve every conflict. It's a necessity to mutually define the issue being worked on and a goal both want to reach. Almost every situation can be better managed using this simple tool. Susan, asking for the trash pickup in the last section, used this technique. Below is another example.

Toni and Matt have been working together on a large and important project. It is time to present it to senior leadership. Both want to present the part on sales projections because it is just what the company has been hoping for. Last year, they and a few others had been in a similar presentation situation that ended in hurt feelings and a great deal of anger. However, Toni and Matt took a class in Ob-Quest.

"Matt, I'd like to present the sales projections. Would you mind if I took that part?

"I think we both know the sales projections are the meat of the presentation and both of us want to do it. Right?"

Toni laughs. "Right. You got any bright ideas?"

"I do. We both worked hard, and I think we both contributed equally. So, why don't we divide the presentation into parts and take turns picking ones we'd like to do. Sort of like, one of us cuts, the other chooses. What do you think?

"You're suggesting we try to divide the glory equally somehow. I think we can do that. Do you have some ideas about how to divide things up?

"Sure do."

It is a lot easier to communicate when trust exists. The best way is to lay your cards on the table, so to speak. Matt did that right off.

I hope that from these examples, you can see how Ob-Quest can work just about anywhere. With practice, you can steer the conversation and problem-solving in the direction you want it to go. You do this by choosing the observation and the question. Trial attorneys do this all the time. So do slick salespeople, psychopaths, and conmen. Statements like, "You can see how buying these windows will save you money," are followed by questions like, "You want to save money, don't you?"

What can you do if Ob-Quest is used against you for evil purposes? First, remember the adage, "You can never cheat an honest man." If you remain honest to the end, the negative uses of this method have little chance to affect you. Second, use the technique yourself. Don't get caught up in the distracting hype of the con artist. Say things like, "I don't understand. Would you explain that again please?"

*   *   *

It is a simple technique, easy to learn and easy to use. You may as well use it today.

How to Say the Impossible

When people talk, listen completely. Most people never listen.
Ernest Hemingway

You know you have horrible news. You've had time to absorb it and know its consequences. The other person doesn't know there is a problem.

What you will say will be a shock, perhaps a terrible shock. You want to communicate so the other person isn't upset.

You cannot make everything okay, even after you've thought about the difficulties of the situation for a while. The best you can do is to present information as well as you can and then help the person handle it.

Follow these steps:

1.   Set the stage
2.   Say your lines
3.   Stop and listen

Setting the stage is like sanding a wall before you paint it. In many situations, it can be as simple as saying, "I have some bad news for you," which is often enough to emotionally prepare the person to hear what you have to say. In other instances, you may have to do more, such as, "My name is Susan Smith and I'm the manager of this department. Something bad has happened and I want to explain it to you. Can we go to my office?"

Say your lines. Tell the person the bad news in one sentence if possible and offer your sympathy. "Your dog escaped from the house this morning, ran into the street, and was hit and killed by a car. I'm very sorry." The more you say after this, the less you communicate. More said at this point is you trying to reduce your own anxiety.

Stop and listen. The person will react. Until the person reacts, you cannot know what to do to help. Stop and listen (and watch) so you know how best to help as the information sinks in. Most often, simply being there to hear and absorb the reaction is the best and most needed thing you can do.

*   *   *

While watching TV or a movie, see how bad news is delivered and think about how you could do it better. Listen to conversations and notice how often people don't stop to let others respond. Balance talking and listening in your communication.

Q and A

Why those skills, Bob?

The ones we looked at will enable you to be independent, improve your perspective of others and to connect with them.

And the ones on problem-solving?

To live your ideal life, you must solve problems as they occur. If you follow the five steps, you're doing all you can to solve a problem, resolve a conflict, and work with others to make the world a better place.

It appears that the five-step problem-solving process might be your favorite skill. Is that true?

It's up there. I think my favorite often changes. The five-steps are so useful and easy to learn, but people seem to forget it almost at once. I wish this could be taught in schools. I sure hope readers teach it to others; that is one great way to learn to use it.

Why include the Men, Women sections? Such a small amount of space for such a big subject.

True. I couldn't cover the entire area and certainly presented stereotypes. My intent was to sketch out the issues.

Where differences exist in gender, age, race and anything else, roots and the wind sneak in. I hope people will realize that and get rid of this tendency.

Can you give us a simple definition of what you mean by "perspective?"

Perspective is the ability to understand the meaning of an event while you're in it or, failing that, as soon as possible. You must have perspective from outside yourself, understand the other people involved and the situation. The way to do that is to be clear about your values and the influence of your roots and the wind.

THE MEANING OF LIFE

OF LIFE

You *and* Others

Become Perfect

Whatever you are, be a good one.
Abraham Lincoln

We began this journey together quoting Plato, "An unexamined life is not worth living." Now it is time to define a life that is worth living. Hold on to your hat, we shall look at the perfect life and see where that gets us. A while ago we said this book wasn't designed to make you a saint. But we never said we wouldn't strive to be something just as lofty. I know it sounds crazy, perfection as a human being. But let's stretch your independence and perspective. Consider the question: Just how good does a person have to be to live an ideal life?

One theme of this book is that outside powers limit your life and weaken self-determination. It is a constant struggle to overcome your roots and the wind. One spectacular way to quiet their ceaseless demands and to live a life of meaning is to become perfect. Why not be perfect? Let's look at achieving the ultimate in life.

Several years ago, I taught a college class in attitude and motivation. Part of the homework for this class was to fill out a workbook entitled "Become Perfect." It took some students almost the entire semester to even consider letting go of old conceptions to accept the new possibilities that were presented. All were buried under a huge root mass.

We all have faults. Our memories are pockmarked with errors, disappointments, failures and regrets. We are flawed, scratched, and dented by the misfortunes of everyday life. "Nobody's perfect," we say to one another with a shrug of our shoulders. The idea is confirmed everywhere, even in fairy tales.

A FAIRY TALE

Once upon a time, in a land far away, there lived a young man and a young woman who were very much in love. He was tall and handsome (too muscular, but this was the olden days) and was the son of the Mayor. She was slim (of course) and beautiful, the favorite daughter of the richest man in town. They were the ideal couple and had been married one year when their child was born. "A marvelous baby," the doctor said, smacking the newborn on the bottom before laying the child in the mother's arms.

The doctor looked at the woman holding her new baby and at the father who was stroking his young wife's hair. His question echoed their thoughts. "Are you going to have your child try the road one day?" he asked.

In this land long ago, on the north side of the village, there was a mysterious road up the mountain and through thick dark stands of trees that everyone was afraid to take. The road was steep and rocky, filled with fearsome monsters and plagued by unimaginable trials.

Generations before, two boisterous brothers had dared each other to take it. One had dared then the other doubled dared. Back and forth they went for weeks until they had to go. One stumbled back after three days.

"It is the road to human perfection," he said. "It was impossible," he added. "I went only a short way before I had to turn back. The climb was too steep, the air too thin to breathe. I tried my best, but it couldn't be done." Everyone nodded. They knew that must be true. Whenever he told his story, which was often, people admired his courage, even though everyone was bored after the first twenty tellings.

The other brother came back after twelve weeks. "It was wonderful," he told the village. "I went all the way to the end and was not what I expected. Most of it was easy. There was not a lot to learn and anyone can do it," he said. "I stayed a while and enjoyed myself before returning."

The villagers were skeptical. He looked no different, talked no different. He smiled a lot though and seemed changed, yet no one could quite understand how. But he couldn't have done it. He must have hidden somewhere. Everyone knew that the road to perfection had to be impossible. Yet, for all his life, friends wondered, for he was a contented man.

The couple knew this story. Everyone in the village knew this story. And if anyone in the village in the last hundred years could attempt the road and become perfect, it would be their child. They looked at one another, then at the doctor. "No," they said. "We love our child and it would be too hard, impossible to take that road. Our baby must stay safe with us, always. We will teach our child what we know to be true and employ the best educators in the land (who all believed that the earth was flat, the world was the center of the universe and that 8,000 fairies could dance on the head of a pin). We will nurture and love with all our hearts. That will enable our child to grow up to be wise and happy."

Like the people in the fairytale village, your parents and everyone who didn't want you to be hurt taught you it is an impossible road. You know and everyone else in the world knows that no one can be perfect. Seeking perfection sounds ridiculous, unbelievable, even irritating. It has been drilled into all of us we are not perfect, and we will never be perfect. Thinking about becoming perfect is absurd.

But wouldn't that be something? To be lying on your deathbed, looking back on your life with a big smile on your face? Remembering all the times it could have been bad, but you made it good? Enjoying one last time the joys and even the sorrows with the people you love? The goal of Personal Wisdom is living the ultimate best life for you. Let's stretch your thinking about human perfection.

THE CONCEPT

The definition of perfection is as if we humans were

machines or spelling tests, instead of thinking, feeling, fun-loving, social creatures. It has not been defined to consider that each of us is unique. And hasn't been defined so at the end of our lives, we can look back without a doubt that we had it right, confident our lives were the absolute best they could be.

Overcome old ways of thinking and embrace the idea that the only way to be perfect is to meet the most important of expectations, your own. And, the only way to meet your expectations is to have reasonable ones, not the unattainable ones promoted every day by people who are not like you.

Is it possible? You be the judge. Becoming perfect is not about developing a great looking body or better hair or a two hundred IQ. Nor is it speaking the King's English in a snooty accent or memorizing a ten-volume encyclopedia, magically getting taller, or even winning a prize for best personality. Perfection is trusting the value of what you already have and making a few adjustments here and there.

The idea is to live a life perfect for you no matter who you are, what your circumstances, what you know, what you have accomplished and how you have failed.

Perfection depends on who is being judged and who is doing the judging. You and only you should establish the standards and decide how you are doing.

The world is fickle, fads come and go, opinions change, the earth continues its path long after we're dead. It's your life. No one else can live it. No one else gets to measure it. It must fit you. And you must get it right the first time.

It has been drilled into you that humans cannot be perfect, and it is impossible to think perfection is even a remote possibility. It's like mocking God or strutting around with disdain for everyone else. What about all those things we're ashamed of, our guilt feelings from now and long ago, our thousands of mistakes?

Each of us knows we are far from flawless. And, none of us like people who act as if they were perfect. They stride about, noses in the air, pontificating as if no one else knows anything and we all wait for them to fall on their rear-ends. Perfection, as we understand it, is a bad idea.

PERFECTION-A GOOD IDEA?

The truth is you've achieved perfection already, quite a few times. Remember the feeling of doing something nice for a stranger or when you fell in love? When you first held your baby? These are perfect moments, an all too brief harmony of you and your surroundings. Perfect moments are those rare events when there is no uncertainty, feelings are pure and powerful, time stands still, beauty is everywhere, we are at one with the universe. We've all had these peak experiences, but never enough. Even these highlights are transitory, not part of what we are.

It is easy for children to have these experiences; the unabashed glee of a first grader watching a Snow White video, finger painting a masterpiece, or, tongue askew, calculating the sum of three and two. Kids can be fully absorbed, without self-consciousness. If we were ever perfect, most people would agree this is the time. What happens? Can we stay perfect? Get it back?

In the attitude and motivation class I taught, I asked students during one of our early meetings if any of them wanted to be perfect. In ten classes of about thirty adult students over three years, no one said "yes." Many said it was impossible and dismissed the idea. Some of the more philosophically minded said it was too hard to define and thus was a meaningless concept. Many objected because becoming perfect would make them different; sterile, like a holy man in a loincloth sitting on a mountain or like the beautiful angel on top of a Christmas tree. Nice. But, no thanks. A substantial number said the concept bordered on sacrilege. Only God can be perfect, any attempt to become so was the devil's work and, like the Tower of Babel, a fool's quest that would end only in disaster. Their roots trapped every one of these students.

Perfection is the measure of the ultimate, the flawless achievement. However, this is not always the case. There are degrees of perfect. In bowling, a three hundred game is the absolute best you can do. But not every ball needs to hit the "pocket." Some balls can miss the ideal spot and still knock down all the pins for the perfect game. A perfect 10 has been achieved in gymnastics, yet slow-motion replays always reveal a few faults. Likewise, a perfect life will include a lot of less than perfect elements.

Imagine walking into the city's best jewelry store with a few million dollars in your pocket. You're about to buy the perfect diamond, with the absolute perfect four Cs, perfect carats, let's say 10 (or 100, whatever size suits you best); perfect color, perfect cut, and perfect clarity.

As a valued customer, you're invited into the locked back room. You're escorted through heavy mahogany doors. The room brightens, lit by golden sconces, two on each dark blue wall. The jeweler motions with his hand for you to sit on a chair upholstered with the finest silks and pulls out a rosewood box from a triple-locked safe. Inside the box, nestled in folds of pale blue velvet, is a huge jewel, glistening, seemingly alive. Holding your breath, you timidly reach in to grasp it and feel the weight of the perfect diamond in the palm of your hand. There is a glow from deep inside, then, as you turn it in your hand, light bursts from every facet like an exploding rainbow. You're mesmerized. You love this stone. It is the most beautiful thing you have ever seen.

Now ask yourself, would that perfect diamond, that

exquisite sparkling gem, the most beautiful thing you have ever seen, make even a halfway decent baseball? What a ridiculous idea. Even if you wanted to throw such a remarkable object, you couldn't throw it very far. It wouldn't roll or bounce off grass and wouldn't connect with a wooden bat with a satisfying crack.

Perfection in a baseball is different from perfection in a diamond. In a baseball, perfection is even stitching, unblemished cowhide, and perfect roundness. Let's say that a young man had such a perfect baseball, kept clean and protected for years in a wooden box he made in high school shop class. Picture him on a summer's eve, professing his love while his girl sways on the front porch swing, a smile betraying her expectations; a little something for her left ring finger.

"Honey," the earnest young man says from on bended knee, "you are the light of my life. Will you marry me?" He fumbles into his coat pocket, pulls out his cherished perfect baseball, and hands it to her. Disaster. She'd either run crying to her room or call Daddy to throw the bum off the porch by the scruff of his neck.

Everything has its own characteristics, those elements that when presented in the optimal fashion, achieve perfection. The characteristics that create perfection in a computer program, for example, are to do the job without errors and as fast as the hardware allows. The characteristics of the perfect computer program are not the same as the characteristics of perfect baseballs or the characteristics of perfect diamonds. Nor are they the same for perfect humans. We are not computer programs, baseballs or diamonds. The first step toward perfection is to find out what perfection is for humans.

Do you think the standards we use to define perfection in a computer program, flawlessness and speed, should apply to people? That would be absurd. Perfection should be defined with criteria appropriate for what we are. We don't need to use nor should we use "flawless" as part of our definition of perfection. That's an impossible to achieve standard, good for computer programs and diamonds, wrong for humans. But I'll bet it was part of what you thought when I first brought up the idea. You may have imagined the perfect person was someone who knew everything and never made a mistake.

When you think about it, we are extraordinarily silly about making mistakes. We define perfection as being unachievable but are ashamed when we make a mistake and often try to deny or hide our faults.

What an impossible dilemma we create, set up by our roots and the wind. We can't think of becoming perfect because that seems impossible, egotistical, sacrilegious or somehow unnatural. We know we are doomed to make mistakes but are compelled by the influences of others to deny them, cover them up, or be embarrassed when others know of them.

Here's a question for you. If you woke up perfect tomorrow, how would you be different from how you are today?

Would you put things like:

1. Never be wrong (It's a hard concept to shake.)
2. Have a great body
3. Rich enough not to worry about anything or anybody
4. Intelligent, not quite Einstein, but very high
5. Powerful, in charge of something important
6. Completely content

We learned our definition of perfection from people like

Mrs. Miller in second grade preaching how important it was to get a hundred percent on the arithmetic test. We received maximum praise for no errors. Most of us got much less encouragement for mere effort or learning. "Nice try, Billy," she would say as she walked by ruffling his hair, "you'll do better next time." (Even though Billy might have stayed up past his bedtime studying and tried his absolute best.)

We learn to keep score and thus self-perpetuate this kind of fallacy. From spelling tests to basketball, from how many boxes of Girl Scout cookies we sell to becoming six-foot-tall, from our income, number of square feet in the house, kind of car, watch, work, and on and on and on, we measure. For each event, there is often, if not always, a sky-high unobtainable measure of perfection.

In high school, one measure of perfection for me was a guy named Brad Stevens. He was captain of the football, basketball and track teams. He ranked in the top five academically, was class president, starred in school plays and musicals, dated the captain of the cheerleaders, and drove his own souped-up car with red flames decorating the hood. And he was as handsome as a movie star. I don't know where he is now, but he may pop up to become President of the United States or a Nobel Prize winner. Brad was my benchmark in high school and I never came close to measuring up. I couldn't accomplish any of the things he could.

But we humans are not events or outcomes, even though we treat ourselves that way. We are always somewhere along the line of a continual personal process of living our individual lives.

Too often, however, we compare ourselves against a measuring stick. Another benchmark I used, this one after college, was writer/producer Michael Crichton. I read an article about him in Parade Magazine and then did a little research. The man wrote a best-selling novel while carving up cadavers as a student at Harvard Medical School and then became a successful Hollywood mogul. I compared myself to him on a list of human characteristics including intelligence, clothes, height, achievements, friends and family, charitable contributions and so on. For everything I thought to put on my list, he was superior, even more so than Brad Stevens. Have you ever done that, found somebody better than you in everything? What a depressing state of affairs. I moped around for days. The space I took up in the world was useless compared to him.

After a while, and it took a while, I began to understand my misperception of the situation. Crichton could do handstands where I could barely walk. But would he? Would Mr. Fantastically Wonderful have the time or the interest to do the things I did to contribute to the world? Would Michael Crichton call *my* mother every Sunday? No, he wouldn't. He wouldn't contribute in any of the ways I did.

So, on one hand, we have the Brad Stevens and Michael Crichtons of the world and on the other, we have the rest of us. What does this mean? It means that there will always be those who do things better, handle situations better, who are our superior in any number of ways. It means there will always be situations when we feel out of place, where we *are* out of place. It also means that feeling second-class is as natural as wincing when you bang your thumb with a hammer.

This feeling of being second class depends on someone else being first class. Most people compare themselves to people who have special talents they don't have. This element of your human nature finds a negative about you and dwells on it. The opposite of this is to make the most of who you are by focusing on what good you do. You need to become your own measuring stick.

That's the crux of the matter. You've heard it a thousand

times. It isn't what someone else can do, or even what your potential is, it is what you do in your own life that means everything. I'm not going to stop a war, discover a cure for AIDS, or build a better mousetrap. But I can say, "I love you," to someone, encourage my children, and call my mother on Sundays. The point is: Live your life your best way, do what is important to you, for those you care about, and for those things you value.

Should your life have less value if on one measure, or on a thousand, you are less than someone else? Should the hawk envy the eagle? An ant the centipede? The ostrich the elephant? You are not the best. You will make mistakes. You have nothing to be ashamed of. What's the point of tomorrow if not to improve on today?

PERFECTION

Is human perfection possible? Can you live a perfect life? With our definition, it sounds like you could, but it also still feels weird. It is difficult to trust you could live your way free from the limits and insecurities the Diabolical Duo has drilled into your head. Pity. Maybe only a lucky few can take the road all the way.

But there remains for all of us something nearly as grand as a perfect life.

Living your ideal life, filled with meaning, is the final step on the road to personal wisdom.

Your
Ideal Life

*Life is about creating
yourself.*
George Bernard Shaw

As a clinician, I was often challenged by the destructive expectations people set for themselves. I talked to a woman who said that all she wanted was to make things a little better for her family and friends and not hurt anyone. We chatted a while about her life and I soon learned why she was always depressed and spent most of her days in bed with the covers pulled over her head.

Her simple goal of doing right for others and not hurting anyone was a need or maybe a compulsion to do the right thing. This woman had learned, however, that everyone had his or her own idea of what was right, often conflicting with her point of view. Yet, she had to be helpful to everybody! If someone wanted a ride to the airport, she was available, even if it meant being late to a promised babysitting job for another friend. She could rarely do what she wanted, and rarely fully satisfy others. Her inability to please everyone was driving her crazy.

Let's take life down a notch from perfect and look at what a best life might be.

THE BEST LIFE...

If you defined best by accomplishments, how many would you need? For years, the United States Ladies Professional Golf Association had a list of accomplishments for their golf Hall of Fame, something like thirty tournament wins including two major titles. (Then they realized nobody could get in.) This human nature element of comparing and competing does the same thing; like finishing college is better than managing only a high school diploma. Women who try to be super-moms or super-women buy into this concept and are plagued by the constant demands of social expectations: Every need must be met every time. Business executives who forget they have a family do this kind of thing at work. Accomplishing things is seductive, an easy way to document value.

Instead of falling into this trap and in the interest of fairness, let's start over and make up new rules on living a best life. How about thirty good deeds a year and two major lifetime contributions to society? If you reach this level of accomplishment, you can count yourself among the best, feel great, and be satisfied with your life. It's a lot like a Boy Scout collecting merit badges to reach Eagle rank.

But this idea wouldn't work. People would disagree on what was a good deed and how they should be counted. Can one good deed balance doing something bad? And anyway, after a while, some do-gooder would form a club for people who did thirty deeds and start charging dues, then somebody else would start a new club for people who did fifty good deeds and design special uniforms only they could wear.

Instead, a good metaphor is that living a best life is like choosing a coat. You could get one off the rack, try it on and if it fit well and looked good, you buy it and wear it. Or you could buy a coat, and have it altered to fit and look good. Maybe you would have a tailor custom make a coat for you. You could even get your coat at a secondhand store. Any of these could provide you with just the right coat for you, but it wouldn't fit other people. Your coat must fit you and please you and doesn't have to fit or please anyone else.

Personal wisdom means having figured out the *ideal* life for you and only you. Your ideal life is a simple and achievable goal—it is the best it can be and is perfect for you.

DEFINING IDEAL

If you are to live your ideal life, you must first define what that is for you. Once you do that, you'll find that living with personal wisdom enables you to live your ideal life.

Below are three criteria that guide my life and that may be useful for you. I created them after years of thinking, wondering, reading, searching, listening, talking, studying, experimenting; doing the best I could to figure out what worked for me and might work for you.

Criterion 1   *Care about yourself and others.*

Caring about yourself is being selfish. This is good, not bad. It's your life, no one else's so you must be the one to make sure you get what you want. As Hillel said, "If I can't be for myself, who can I be for?"

I define caring about myself in several ways, some

contradictory. For example, I enjoy a glass of Scotch most evenings. In the short run, this gives me much pleasure. I know, however, that I would be better off in the long run if I got off my chair and out of the house to run a mile or two. Which is better? It's my choice. I will care about myself in ways that work for me, not necessarily anyone else.

However, Hillel also said, "If I am only for myself, what kind of man can I be?" I owe so much to others I can never repay my debt. Caring about others is a duty and a privilege. Caring about others means listening well to overcome your personal biases so you can respond in the right way to meet others' needs.

Caring about yourself *and* others is a challenge, one I sometimes fail to meet. I have learned that it is easier for me to sacrifice my own desires. I hate disappointing or hurting friends and family. The balance between caring about yourself and others changes all the time. The idea is for you to do both as well as you can.

For many, the primary source of joy is connecting with others. This can occur only if you are honest and open, true to yourself and dedicated to the welfare of others. Me *and* you works for me.

Criterion 2   *Admit to making an error as soon as you know you have made one and fix it as well as you can.*

Making a mistake seems to be a horrible thing to do. Our society punishes mistakes rather than views them as a chance to learn. Society has gone wrong somewhere. I don't know of anyone who wants to make a mistake; or anyone who doesn't make a bunch of them.

For the longest time, I hated making mistakes. I wanted to be flawless. I didn't have to be the best, just a person no one could find fault with. As I've gotten older, I've learned from the limitations of age. No longer must I be able to do everything. I can admit to not having the strength to open a pickle jar, to not being able to program a new electronic gadget and can admit to forgetting things. I still don't like making errors, but they no longer define my self-worth.

As I've learned to do the first part, admitting to an error, the second has become easy. Only I must make sure that as I fix my mistakes, I do two things, repair the damage to others as well as I can, and then forgive myself and move on. No need to make excuses. No need to wallow. I do my best to get on with my life; which is part of criterion number one, caring about yourself.

Criterion 3   *Always be working toward personally fulfilling goals.*

Like many people of retirement age, I wonder what I should do when I no longer trundle off to work. I want my life to have purpose when I roll out of bed in the morning. My dad enjoyed playing golf with his friends three times a week. I don't think that will work for me. I want to feel I am contributing in some useful way. My job with this principle is to monitor what I am doing to make sure I am always working toward meaningful goals.

The reason behind this criterion is that we humans are goal oriented. A satisfying life comes from taking control of this attribute and making it work for you. Define what is meaningful and significant to you. Do things, perhaps every day that help you achieve these goals.

Your ideal life is one that minimizes wishing you had done things differently. The only way to do this is to have clear and personally meaningful goals. You can change them as you go along, but you must have somewhere to aim.

Having meaningful goals takes many forms. Worshiping every week or every day and honoring God with thought and action is one. Working toward making the Olympic team is another. Doing a good deed every day is yet a third. Even learning how to sit in the shade of a tree and nap is a reasonable goal. You can have long-term goals combined with dozens of objectives that may take a lifetime to reach, or intermediate and short-term goals that stand alone. You can reach them, or perhaps change your mind and seek something else. The important part is that they are meaningful to you and you are working toward them.

The ideal life must include the goal of achieving a sense of meaning; otherwise, what's the point of getting out of bed in the morning? Hidden in our three criteria for an ideal life is the meaning of life.

One concept that best encompasses all three criteria is contributing, to you, others, and something outside yourself.

THE IDEAL YOU

Personal Wisdom is not like an expensive watch you can wave under people's noses or some framed certificate with ribbons and golden glitter you hang on your den wall. Living your ideal life is not knowing everything but understanding yourself. It is becoming part of everyone, not standing on a pedestal. When you live with personal wisdom, you will be humble, willing to stand aside, listen, and learn.

There is an old saying: "Before enlightenment, I chopped wood and carried water. After enlightenment, I chopped wood and carried water."

When you are wise, no one else will know. They'll sense something has changed, though. They may ask if your hair is different.

The best way to understand personal wisdom is that it is

not a state of being, but a process, like walking through a beautiful garden or enjoying a kiss. It comes and goes like everything else, but once you feel it, it is yours. The result is that you will live a life that is satisfying, fulfilling, and productive; one of meaning and one that is perfect for you.

When you are living your ideal life, you will know that each day was as good as it could be, and that tomorrow will be better. You will be living your values and creating a life that means something, and it will be a good one.

*   *   *

Keep in mind the three criteria are whats, not hows. For one person, caring your yourself might mean taking a death-with-dignity pill when a disease becomes overwhelming. For another, caring for yourself might mean fighting the disease with every fiber her being until her savior welcomes her home. You became independent so you can choose the right decision for you, and only you.

The Meaning of Life

...the meaning of life differs from man to man, from day to day and from hour to hour.
Viktor Frankl

There is no shortage of ideas on how to live a meaningful life. Joshua Marine says it's overcoming obstacles. For Thomas Merton love is the answer. Revering God is found almost everywhere from holy books to self-help manuals. Arnold Schwarzenegger suggests the meaning of life is to achieve, to conquer. Way back to Aristotle it was happiness. Many say it is following our dreams. An equal number say it is facing our challenges. Living with purpose resonates with many people today. Picking yourself up from failure is also popular.

So, what is it? What is the meaning of life?

MEANING IS DUAL

So far, we have covered *Life, You, Others,* and *Life Skills*. It's time to put our findings into action. To have one meaning for all these elements would seem to be impossible, but that is what we will do, but only after we agree to two concepts.

Concept number one is that the meaning of life is unique to each individual and the meaning of life must define the ideal life for that person.

Concept number two is that the meaning of life must be outside the person and include some higher purpose important to the individual and others.

The meaning of life is a dual meaning; you *and* others. They must be separate, but one without the other is meaningless.

And there is a second duality, whether or not the person believes in God. There are arguments that without God, moral life and moral society is impossible. But thinkers such as Benjamin Franklin, Thomas Jefferson, Emily Dickinson, Mark Twain and Thomas Edison support the contention that moral people and moral society can exist without a belief in God. For some the choice is clear, for others, it takes considerable effort to decide. We'll look at both.

GOD EXISTS

For those who believe in God, life promises to be a way station to paradise. For almost every current religion, God has created a life-after-death beyond our comprehension. It wasn't always that way. Before the God of Abraham, gods did not promise everlasting life nestled in benevolent arms. But He has for those alive now and reading this book.

One problem is which god is the right one to believe in. There are many choices.

For most people, the god they believe in was an accident of birth. Where you were born and to whom made the difference. Even a change in religious belief most often occurs when a person moves to an area of differing belief or becomes connected with someone from a different religion.

My answer to which god is the right god is that it doesn't matter. To me, God is the same God with the only difference being how you obey and worship Him. This belief will be wrong to everyone who follows a specific religion, but it makes sense to me.

What didn't make sense to me was heaven. Eternity is a long time and I couldn't figure out how a place, no matter how fantastic, wouldn't become boring after say the first 50,000,000,000,000 years. That bothered me. I asked people about it and the answers I got were not much help; things like, "Oh, His eternal light will keep you happy." That sounded too much like being on a drug high for eternity.

Being of a scientific mind, I sought understanding through logic. When I began to understand the theory of relativity, where time and space are interconnected and not constant, I put together a concept of heaven that made sense to me.

I like the idea of two or three heavens. The first heaven is one that everyone designs in their own heads, based on their beliefs while alive. It's a different heaven for everyone. My first heaven is one where I am free to go anywhere and be anyone I want to be. I can be myself and meet famous people or I can be that famous person. That sounds like fun for a while.

The second heaven would be something I think God would create. I don't know what it would be, but something fantastic. I would stay there until boredom set in.

The third and final heaven would be the real one, the one God designed. Here, time, that constant on earth, would change. Time would either stop or somehow not exist at all. I don't know what that would be like, but it allows heaven to make sense to me. (This idea led to the novel, *My First Ten Days in Heaven*.)

GOD DOES NOT EXIST

Those who don't believe in a creator have a big problem. Believing in God makes life purposeful, do the right thing and enjoy everlasting life. With no god, what's the point?

According to many non-believers, the point is to create meaning.

As my friend humanist Jim Corbett would say a person must understand the difference between the meaning *of* life and the meaning *in* life. Let me explain how I see the difference.

The meaning *of* life asserts either human life itself is inherently meaningful, or an individual's life, one life, is potentially meaningful. The subtlety here is that the meaning *of* a single life necessitates a judgment at the end of life, declaring it had meaning or not.

Life has meaning if you did good deeds and went to heaven. If you failed to do good deeds and did not go to heaven, your life would not have meaning. The definition of good deeds would depend on your religion.

Although death is scary for most people, knowing that you followed the teachings of your religion would provide comfort that you would pass judgment when you died, and enter a much better existence, no matter how unknown it might be. That is the just reward for those seeking the meaning *of* life; a reverence for your creator in the right ways.

The meaning *of* life is in the reward after death. Meaning *in* life requires a judgment of a much different kind. This kind of meaning assumes that death ends possibilities and that meaning must be found in life, along the way. It is the good deeds during life, however they are defined, that create meaning *in* life.

Just like believers, nonbelievers must (or should, anyway) decide what they believe in and do what than justifies their existence according to those standards. There is no paradise waiting at the end. You do good things because good things are the right things to do.

Without a grand award at the end, many people make the mistake of believing their lives should tell a story, one with a beginning, a middle and an end. The image of the most satisfying end is lying in a deathbed at home, not being afraid, in fact, enjoying a sense of contentment and a life well-lived, while sharing last bits of wisdom and goodbyes with loved ones. Rarely does this happen. Those that need it this way will be disappointed.

The best thing to do if you are a nonbeliever is to define your meaning, do what you have defined, assume life is a series of events and one of those events will be the end of your life and that will be it. Derive your meaning *in* your life, not by your ending or pleasing story arc.

A GOOD LIFE

Life is like playing baseball. No matter how hard you try, no matter how good you are, you will strike out sometimes, drop the ball, be tagged out at home. Life is going to rear up and smack you hard; as hard and mean and painful as getting hit in the face by a fastball. Life will bring you to your knees and make you wonder why you were ever born. But, no matter how badly you swing the bat, misjudge a fly ball, or stumble toward home plate, you just might hit a home run, catch the ball you lost in the sun, or slide under the tag. No matter what mistakes you make, you can end up winning.

Let's take a quick inventory. You're not perfect, right? (Trick question.) You could stand to shed a few pounds, maybe. Sometimes you lose your temper, forget to run an errand, hurt somebody's feelings. You have leaped to conclusions, rushed to judgment, fallen for a smooth line. You would probably admit you could benefit from extra polishing.

You could be a little nicer on the freeway, try harder to be friendly, or telephone your friends more often. You would be a better person if you watched less TV, read more great books, volunteered at the homeless shelter, said you were sorry a little more often.

Yet, you only have so much time, so much energy. You can't do everything. You don't *want to* do everything. You are all for living a better life but are not willing to lie on a couch being analyzed two hours a day for five years to learn how to do it. Nor do you want to improve just anything. It would be nice to learn a new language, or study the Koran, Bible, or other holy books, or even learn more about how vitamins work. What things would add to your life, make it more enjoyable, and ensure a sense of contentment?

A satisfying life requires two elements; making good choices, ones that feel good and turn out right, and adjusting well to whatever happens when things go wrong. Making good decisions is difficult.

You need enough knowledge. You also need to be clear thinking. Unbiased observations would help. And the honest acknowledgment of consequences also lends itself to good decision-making. So does adjusting to life as needed.

Adjusting to events means recognizing that life is not fair. It's realizing and accepting that you're not the center of the universe. Adjusting is understanding that sometimes the best you can do is accept life on its terms.

THE BIG QUESTION

When I was growing up, the English gentleman was my hero; Ronald Coleman or James Bond, it didn't matter who. (Talk about the wind. My early identity was created from my visit to Scotland when I was ten, British movies and a few books about the Royal Air Force, Lawrence of Arabia and James Bond.) I wanted to be cool under fire, win Wimbledon without breaking a sweat, lecture in physics at Cambridge without notes, and play Albert Hall with the London symphony.

I had to sweep beautiful women off their feet with charm, wit, and ruggedly handsome features; order a ten-course dinner in any of a dozen languages; know the vintage, chateau, and harvest temperature of every wine; and smoke cigars that had been rolled on the sweaty thighs of exotic dark-haired mountain girls. I would smile at adversity and laugh at danger.

I soon realized that I would never be 007 or even secret agent Austin Powers. I was as middle-of-the-road normal and common as anyone born and raised in the American Midwest could be, middle-class standards, suburban house, two parents and two siblings, a one-car garage, basement rec room, playing with the neighbor kids, getting an occasional "A" on a test. I was just a regular guy.

Life was straightforward except late at night when everyone else was asleep, and thoughts of life and death made my throat tighten and my heart pound.

Except when I saw my mother cry or when the man next door shot himself and was carried out covered with a sheet, leaving a pool of blood on the basement floor we saw through the casement window.

Except when my grandmother left our family to marry a stranger back in the old country or when I wondered where heaven was and who was there and what would they do all day, every day, week after week, year after year, for all eternity.

I wondered how life made sense and fell into a limited understanding of what was important from what I learned from others. At Sunday school, the minister told us to trust God and patted us all on the head. During science class, Mr. Himlin preached evolution, survival of the fittest, and the end of the universe. A friend offered me a joint and said that here were all the answers. Television announced that I only go around once in life, so I should grab all the gusto I could. Linda Sneed kissed me on the mouth and got me totally weird. The philosopher John Paul Sartre told me life was absurd, but I was responsible for what I did, anyway. The Bomb was dropped a year before I was born. I was vaccinated for polio just after the Korean War and drafted during Vietnam.

For years I wondered what I was supposed to do with this life that accidentally came my way. Should I follow the old and the wise, march in my own parade, or live with a shrug of the shoulders and another glass of wine?

When would I know enough to make the best decisions? What if, at the very edge of slipping into that long dark night, I realized with wide-eyed horror I had done it wrong?

THE MEANING OF LIFE

Here is how to make sure you don't do it wrong. It is time to define the one, true, right for everyone, meaning of life. A quest more important than understanding the universe, it is the key to your ideal life, the reason to get out of bed in the morning, the spark that makes life worth living, the why of every breath we take. The human value that has been the holy grail of philosophers, saints, scientists, teachers, mothers and kings for thousands of years and has inspired, saddened, confused, hurt or made whole every human that ever lived.

The meaning of life is why your roots were grown and why you had to examine them and is why so many people bend to the wind. The meaning of life is what makes sense of everything.

Here it is: *Contribute*

This means, in your own way, you contribute* to God, country, humankind, yourself, the environment, your family, anything you wish.

Teach a kid to swim, open a door for someone, run for political office. Large or small, you contribute to the world outside you to make a difference.

With personal wisdom, you know what is true for you. You appreciate and endorse the value of others. You make choices that are the absolute best ones you can make.

To contribute sounds too easy. It is easy, but why not? Everyone should be able to do it. Everyone should be able to enjoy a meaningful life.

The only question that remains is: How much?

What is contributing enough to have meaning?

How will you know if you're doing even this simple task the right way?

How good do you have to be to do good?

You get to decide. Sometimes it will be not so much; other times it will be a lot. Contribute what you want to, contribute what you can.

---

* The scientifically minded might want to define "contribute" as reversing entropy for a while.

Q and A

Why the concept of "Perfect?"

Not much is more ingrained in us than we are fallible and thus unable to know what is best for us. I wanted to smash that barrier to your ideal life by making our human fallibility irrelevant and make self-defined perfection as something to think about.

People cringe at the idea of human perfection; it seems to be automatically rejected. But that's the point of this book; don't automatically do anything if you can help it unless you know your automatic response is the best one for you.

Why those three elements for an ideal life?

An ideal life must fit each individual. I spent over three decades sorting out possibilities. The three I chose are right for me, can be adjusted by you and others as needed, and are few and simple enough to make sense. However, you may want more than three, or less, or different ones. But I think it is necessary to define them.

Can everyone achieve personal wisdom?

I'm not sure. I think it may take more imagination and maturity and more humility than some people have. Living your ideal life is a subtle thing too, and that may be hard for some.

The End

The End

> *I expect to pass through this world but once; any good thing therefore that I can do, or any kindness that I can show to any fellow creature, let me do it now; let me not defer or neglect it, for I shall not pass this way again.*
> Ettiene De Grellet

There have been two major themes running through this book. One is the importance of contributing; an individual choosing to invest in something bigger than just one life. This could be donating to a charity, devoting yourself to your faith or sacrificing your life for a cause you believe in.

The other theme is to be brave, to go beyond the common framework of your life to soar over mountains to unknown adventures. When you entered the world, you were gifted the opportunity to contribute something unique to the universe. I don't think anyone, God or man, wants you to just rehash what came before you, grounded by your roots and weaving in the wind. Your life should count for something, and that something should be of your choosing.

You have worked hard with this book. You have taken a sometimes-difficult look at who you are and what you want. I hope you have learned lessons of value. I have one last idea.

In defining goals to work toward, one goal may be more important and useful than any of the rest. The goal is to live so that certain words may be written on your tombstone.

What I would want to be written on mine is:

His was an enjoyable and useful life.

Decide what you want to be written on yours and live so it can happen.

Be a unique being in the universe, be an important somebody in the grand scheme of things—be you.

Q and A

Do you have any last words on making sense of me, others and the meaning of life?

I do, but they are not my words. These are from a graduate school professor, George Valhos. They might bring together everything we have talked about. As part of our personal and professional development, he asked us to answer four questions.

1. Who are you?

2. Who are others?

3. Why are you?

4. Why are others?

Personal Truths at the back of the book is a final section if you wish to further explore who you are.

GLOSSARY

Become
Perfect

Human perfection is actually possible
(but not so popular) because it is a
moment, not an outcome.

Death

The end of all possibilities—except how
we influenced others.

Defining Moments

The consequences of what you decide and
then do.

Goals

Guides toward success as you continue to
move past them.

Hope

One of the primary emotions that allows
you to be imperfect on your journey and
to accept the injuries and injustices of life.
It also can motivate you to make things
better.

Independence

The ability and willingness to define
yourself and take responsibility for who
you are and what you do.

Intimacy

A sense of connectedness to another
person or even a group, culture or nation.
This is one of the highest achievements
and benefits of life.

Life

The only time when you can create who
you are. It is your chance to feel joy and
contribute to the well-being of the
universe.

Love	When the welfare of another is more important than your own. This can be measured in an almost infinite number of degrees, often a blending of passion, intimacy and commitment.
Meaning of Life	Contributing value through deeds and love.
Others	Everyone is different. Your job is to make that a good thing.
Personal Truths	A more concrete way for you to decide who you want to be and can act as a guide or checklist.
Personal Wisdom	The degree that you live your life independent of everyone and anyone else, learning and adding value to others as you do.
Perspective	Freely understanding yourself, others, and the meaning of life.
Roots	Your foundation, the source of your basic beliefs. They can and should give you stability. They can also keep you in one place. You have choices.
Rules	Obligations you didn't ask for—unless you created them yourself.
Skills	Acquiring the ability to live your ideal life effectively.
True Knowledge	What you have learned to be true through your personal, unique and unbiased experience.

You	You have two significant questions to answer in life:

1. Who am I?
2. What am I going to contribute?

Value	Making things better, especially for others. Simply put, do something to improve the world, from picking up a piece of trash to raising a child.
Vision	Being able to see beyond the ordinary, to see yourself and the rest of the world in perspective.
Wind, the	The ebb and flow of popular opinion, what's in, what's out. It's the combined force of everyone's roots and insecurities. It is always blowing.
Wisdom	According to Marcel Proust, "We don't receive wisdom; we must discover it for ourselves after a journey that no one can take for us or spare us."
Worth	The starting point for humans and many other living things.
Worthiness	A sense of self that is a good gauge of your value only if it is not driven by the wind and only if it results in the well-being of others.

ACKNOWLEDGEMENTS

Over the thirty-five years I worked on this book, there were many people who offered suggestions or taught me things I could add.

I learned a lot from those I saw in my clinical practice and I thank them. The organizations for which I was a consultant also contributed to my greater understanding of how life works—and doesn't work.

My two children, who arrived as young teens when I married Deena, test out my theories every time I see them. So far, so good, they say.

My parents and my sister Barb (and her husband Dan) and my brother Bill (and his wife Sue) added to my understanding of how the world operates. Barb and Dan are proponents of doing things the tried and true way. My brother was more of a "my way" kind of guy. Both have been good teachers.

My father taught me many lessons, some of which I have included in the book. My mother, who was the type of Mom who could slip a rubber egg sandwich into my brown bag school lunch, had the greatest impact on my early understanding of the world. Dear friend Jim Hay has always tried to help me understand reality (with some success).

Other guys, Brent Maynard and Mark Maynard and Nick Colovus contributed to my understanding of friendship. Another, my old friend Robin Halley, helped me comprehend all the sides of adversity and what gentleness of spirit means.

Laura McDowell read an early version, typed much of it from a barely legible scrawl, and added considerable insights including tell the truth, but not always be telling it.

My friend Jim Corbett, who thinks outside the box almost all the time, is helping me to make things happen much more than I thought possible.

Malcolm Ferrier (and his wife Wendy) also kept me on my toes to make sure I expressed my ideas clearly (and did the final editing of the first edition).

I was first exposed to concepts of problem-solving in graduate school by Professor Roger Kaufman. We spent an entire semester applying his ideas to every conceivable issue. I applied them to the psychotherapy process for my dissertation. His thinking has been a very important factor in my work.

Several others have contributed to the ideas in this book, too many to mention by name. However, a few that have looked at various versions are Deborah Borowski, Erin Reid, Carolyn Cone, Beckie Stewart, Alice Thabar, Nancy Neil, my friend and co-author Rudy Williams, Annette Nitz, and many members of the Whidbey Island Writers Group.

Jann Carpenter, who I consider a mentor, read one version overnight, then provided page after page of notes and ideas. I have used many of them, and fear that the book would be much better if I had used them all.

Psychologist, writer and active environmentalist Bob Rich did the initial editing. His breadth of knowledge and attention to detail found every error I made, and his suggestions were right on the mark.

Then there is Kathleen Bailey who recently reviewed the book and wrote a note suggesting improvements in layout among other suggestions. Her thoughts led me to create an updated edition.

My wife, Deena, who has been with me for almost the entire effort, has given me both love and an often much-needed bonk on my head when I become too full of my own ideas.

PERSONAL
TRUTHS

A mini workbook for those who want to further
explore their ideal life

Personal Truths

We've arrived at a most substantial portion of our effort to live our personal best, and this is the last time we can discuss your life. Please keep in mind the importance of separating yourself from your roots, that mass of human history you have joined, and the wind that buffets you, all those daily pushes and prods that may not be right for you. If you had been born in Massachusetts 400 years ago, you would have believed in and been afraid of witches. Born 200 years later in Japan, you would have believed in and died for your emperor-god. Today, a lot of your beliefs are also accidents of the time and place of your birth. Think about how different you would be if you were born Catholic or Protestant in Northern Ireland in 1950 or black in Mississippi in 1910 or female in China in 1890. You must define who you are and what you stand for by true knowledge, not right opinion that our friend Plato warned us about quite a few years ago.

The only way to live your ideal life is to be independent of the herd. There is no formula, no right way, no script except the one you write. Each of us must take ultimate responsibility for what we have done and what we will do. Many religions have us arriving before God after death, reporting on our lives, and being judged for our deeds and misdeeds. Before that happens, you must do the same thing for yourself. You must create your own Personal Truths.

Personal Truths comprise your life, each moment added together forming your years and your accomplishments. Personal Truths is a collection of your decisions, actions, feelings and hopes, your impact on others, your intentions and consequences. It is the trail you leave after your passage and the memories within others. It is your book and much of it has yet to be written. There is no eraser, but there is always a new blank page.

What you will create is like a diary in that it's an intimate portrait, but not like any diary you've seen before. It does not reflect your past as much as it is your vision of your future. It prepares you for living your best today by helping you understand your yesterdays and define your tomorrows.

The remaining pages outline important elements of creating your Personal Truths. Create your truths so you can make sure you are taking care of yourself and others in the way most important to you.

Make sure you choose your role on life's stage and you write your lines the way you want them to be. Choose other categories if you like and add to the categories in any way you wish.

This is your guidebook to your life.

Review your Personal Truths occasionally to monitor how you are doing. It is much like looking in on the baby or checking the oil level in your car. You must check to make sure things are okay. The same idea holds true when you are creating and living your ideal life.

We have been working on your perspective, so you can recognize a defining moment even while the Diabolical Duo is trying to hide it. You can use your personal wisdom, values, perceptions, even flip a coin to make the right decisions for you. From now on, little that is important will escape your notice. When a child reaches out a hand, when the sun dips behind a cloud, when you listen to a friend, you'll appreciate the moment. And each of your important moments will be yours.

One last thought. As you do your best with your life and you meet with others of your global village, share your wisdom.

INSTRUCTIONS

Write in pencil, always. Write on these pages or in a notebook, three-ring binder, eBook or your computer so you can look at it occasionally. Add these new ideas to your prior notes or edit the earlier entries as you wish.

While I recommend working on the following pages, you don't have to. For some, this effort would be a waste of valuable time, work that doesn't add value. For others, the degree of detail is necessary to become your best.

PERSONAL TRUTHS

Date _____

List ten of your most important values.

1.

2.

3.

4.

5.

6.

7.

8.

9.

10.

List your major life-long goals. (For me, one of them is to write an important book.)

1.

2.

3.

4.

5.

6.

7.

8.

9.

10.

List your goals for the next five to ten years. (One of mine is to visit Alaska.)

1.

2.

3.

4.

5.

6.

7.

8.

9.

10.

List your goals for the next one to five years. (For me, create a final will.)

1.

2.

3.

4.

5.

6.

7.

8.

9.

10.

List your defining moments. Don't list more than five unless you feel compelled to do so. Describe the moment, when it happened and what it means. If it means something negative to you, return to the goals section and create a goal of creating a different perspective of the event. (By being with each of my parents as they died, I gained added perspective on the fragility of life and honor them and life even more.)

1.

2.

3.

4.

5.

List things that give you a sense of identity, the roles you play and what gives you self-esteem. (When I write, I feel I'm doing my best to contribute to the world.)

1.

2.

3.

4.

5.

6.

7.

8.

9.

10.

Write your relationship rules in four categories, as a friend, intimate partner, parent, and child.

Friend:

1.

2.

3.

4.

5.

Intimate Partner:

1.

2.

3.

4.

5.

Parent:

1.

2.

3.

4.

5.

Child:

1.

2.

3.

4.

5.

Write your rules for being a member of society.

1.

2.

3.

4.

5.

List your rules for creating meaning in your life.

1.

2.

3.

4.

5.

Now let's take a good look at your roots and the wind.

GENDER RULES

A set of very personal rules and ones certainly used every day are sex-role rules. In some places, boy babies wear blue hats and girl babies wear pink ones. In other places, adult women are covered head to toe and men aren't. Some cultures encourage differences others reinforce similarities. These rules are of great interest today and large segments of the world are closely evaluating old rules and making up new ones. Listing yours should be easy, interesting, and enlightening.

Gender rules should:

1. Relate you to others of your sex
2. Contrast you to others of the opposite sex
3. Define many of your actions and expectations

You may not need any help with these, but here are two common ones anyway:

"As a man, I should do more of the dirty work."

"As a woman, I am more nurturing."

On the next page, begin the process of ensuring your Roots and the Wind allow you to go where you want to go.

ROOTS AND THE WIND

Gender Rules: As a _____ (man or woman):

1.

2.

3.

4.

Did you discover anything interesting? If you listed rules stating that the sexes were equal, I think you were writing a social rule rather than a gender one. Did any of your rules say anything about attracting a sexual partner or regarding physical differences? Any mention of expressing feelings? Most would agree that men as a group seem to be more interested than women in tangible, logical things and getting to a goal ("Ah, she won't want flowers. I'll get her a vacuum cleaner for our anniversary.").

Women appear to understand feelings better and be more involved in the process of interactions between people. Did you include that sort of difference for yourself? Look at your list again and erase what you want to change or add other rules as you think are needed. (You did this in pencil, didn't you?)

PARENTAL RULES

Highly impervious to change are parental rules. These rules are from parents, guardians, adult authorities, or even wise older children. A good friend of mine got this one from his father: "If you have to do something, do it quick and cheap. Don't waste your time overdoing it." I don't know if his father said that, but even today my friend tends to finish projects quickly and sometimes without the effort they deserve. If he's constructing a bookshelf at home, for example, he will often use scrap wood that he found lying around the basement and other materials ill-suited for the project. He says he does this to reduce the cost and to get the job done quicker. It drives his wife crazy.

Rules from my father:

1.

2.

3.

Rules from my mother:

1.

2.

3.

Rules from other adults or wiser older children:

1.

2.

3.

Are any of these no longer good? Write any new ones that you want to live by now. If you have kids, make sure your parental rules are in their best interests. Use a new category, "New Parental Rules (or better interpretations of the old ones)" and list those if you have some.

New Parental (or Grand-parental) Rules

1.

2.

3.

4.

AGE RULES

Another set of rules, like gender rules, are age rules. You remember that at sixteen you should have had a driver's license or, at sixty-five, be ready to retire. In sixth grade, we should be ready to discover the opposite sex. At 18, or perhaps 22, we should be ready to get a job or be married. Or did you have different rules? Age rules should:

1. Define the age, either a specific age or span of time.
2. Include you in an age group or keep you separate.
3. Define some sort of achievement or behavior now or by a certain time in the future.

Here's an example: "At age 60 I should own my home and have a lot of money socked away for retirement."

Let's do it. Write out your age and list three rules you operate from because you're that age.

Age rules for me at age _____:

1.

2.

3.

It might be interesting to ask others what one of their age rules is.

Let's do some self-analysis using the concept of age rules. It's probably safe to assume that age rules change as you age. So, let's look at age rules through time.

First, here are two examples that probably applied to all of us. Rules for a one-year-old:

1. These people who feed me are all-powerful.
2. Life is not acceptable if I'm cold, hungry, or wet.
3. I can sleep whenever I want to.
4. Etc.

Rule as a four-year-old:

I know everything.

You are probably aware that we grow up through a series of stages, such as the terrible twos, that are partly due to physical and mental growth and partly due to our own life experience.

For practice and perhaps a little enlightenment, list two of your past age rules as you can recall them. Think about how you might have been, how you acted, how you felt about yourself, your relationship to your parents and teachers, what you enjoyed doing, and what you didn't like.

Rules for me as a 10-year-old:

1.

2.

3.

Did you learn anything? (If you didn't, you may want to compare what you wrote to what a real live ten-year-old would write.)

Are there any rules you wish had been different? I remember one rule for me was:

"Don't do anything wrong, bad, or unsafe."

It seems like a pretty good rule for a kid, but what it caused for me was a shy personality and not a whole lot of chance taking. Because of this rule, there was a late start learning how to ride a two-wheeler and a lot of other behaviors that I either was late doing or didn't get to. Mostly though, there was an avoidance of failure and therefore little stretching of my limits. Make sure you know the consequences of your rules.

What about when you were twenty? List a couple of age rules for you then.

Rules for me as a 20-year-old:

1.

2.

Let's go in the other direction, into the future. Design how you would like to be five years from now. Add five years to your current age and list two rules you would like to have when you become that age, different from ones you have now.

Rules for me 5 years from now:

1.

2.

Done? Good. I hope you can be and do these things.

Please do one more listing. Write down a couple of the rules you would like to have when you are old, however you define that. (Personally, I define old age as when you no longer anticipate the joy of discovering something new—I hope I never get there.)

Rules for me near the end of my life:

1.

2.

Would any of these be good rules to follow now?

SYMBOLIC RULES

These rules are immensely powerful and are based on thin air. Take the case of our anorexic friend Mary Ann; a small number on the bathroom scale meant all was right in the world and a higher number meant she was an out-of-control fat slob whom everyone despised. This is a symbolic rule.

Clothes are symbolic, obviously. Language is. You belong to or are excluded from groups by your words and phrases. Your car (or pick-up), house, watch, almost everything is or could be, symbolic. Whenever you decide, if there is more than one reason for it, often one of the reasons is symbolic. Are you wearing any jewelry right now? Is it symbolic? Are some of the magazines left out on your coffee table for show? What's your reaction when someone cuts you off on the freeway? Do you think you may be defending symbolic territory in a symbolic way?

Arguments are mostly symbolic and usually about domination issues. When combatants finally calm down, they often wonder, "What were we fighting about anyway?" This is a clear clue of a symbolic interaction. Jobs can be symbolic. Some blue-collar workers wear ties to work before changing into coveralls at the job. How you drive can be. What you do Friday nights can be. List some of your symbolic rules and what the pay-off is. I've included an example of one that I've seen in action.

Symbolic rule: Seatbelts are for sissies.

Payoff: I am viewed as tough, independent, powerful, hip, carefree, etc. etc.

So, write two or three symbolic rules and their payoffs.

Symbolic behavior rules:

1.

Payoff:

2.

Payoff:

3.

Payoff:

There is nothing wrong with symbolic interaction. Governments, the military, societies, and most other human institutions run on symbolic interaction (the boss runs the meetings even though someone else might do it better), symbolic behavior ("snappy salute there, corporal"), and symbolic pay-offs ("What a marvelous bowling trophy!"). The important thing is to know the real value of the symbol and be aware that a social symbol can become more important than the individual's value. Braving machinegun fire to protect one's flag is one example. Another is wearing very uncomfortable shoes because they are the current style. Make sure to know when you are following a symbolic rule and what the payoff is.

ETHNIC RULES

Another mega-powerful Diabolical Duo element is race, ethnicity, and nationality. Let's continue to expose your roots and the wind by listing two of the major rules of your ethnic or racial background that define who you are supposed to be.

This is difficult, I know, so here are two examples of me, a first-generation American of two Scots parents.

1. Scots strongly believe in thrift.
2. Scots have the most moving music in the world.

Notice any prejudice in these statements? The second one appears to be a rule learned while growing up listening to bagpipes in all their glory. Often such a bias remains strong because the person has not experienced anything that would change it. Racial prejudice, for example, if you don't like blacks, whites, yellows, or greens and you don't ever positively interact with blacks, whites, yellows, or greens because of your bias, you won't change. Prejudice is a self-perpetuating loop of ignorance and avoidance.

List two major ethnic rules instilled in you by what you were taught or experienced. Do not write down rules as you think they should be. List the rules as you sense they are for you.

For those of you with no clear ethnic background, use

whatever you have, or what the lack of such a background means. Or, if you want, write rules based upon regional expectations (e.g. a California girl or good ol' Southern boy). What I want you to write are the ethnic or racial generalizations or stereotypes that define you.

Make sure you are not just listing observations. List the rules (or stereotypes) that guide your attitudes and behavior. That's the only way to be able to decide if the rule is right for you or not.

My current ethnic rules:

1.

2.

The basic rules that control you are partly defined by society and partly by your perceptions. No matter how society may define rules, there is an infinite range of refinements you can make. Some of yours may be contrary to society's, others well within accepted limits.

Take a good look at the backdrop society has designed for your role. Everything else you become either contrasts with or matches these rules.

Unfortunately, some ethnic rules are used to treat others as outsiders and therefore exploitable. From fleecing tourists at small-town speed traps to "charity begins at home" to genocide, regional, ethnic, and racial rules can justify any kind of treatment of those who are different. So-called "ethnic cleansing" campaigns have emanated from these rules to the shame of us all.

Now that you have listed what you think are the two major, overall ethnic rules for you, list two additional ethnic rules.

Each of your rules should do one or both of two things:

1. Define you as a member of a group.
2. Compare you to members of your group or other groups.

Two examples of someone living in the American south might be:

1. I am black, and I will treat everyone the same, no matter what their color.
2. In some places, I still must fight for my rights.

Write a couple that are true for you.

1.

2.

Various cultures have different ways of handling insults or injuries from others. Some advocate peacemaking by turning the other cheek while others seek revenge, vowing an eye for an eye. And while some cultures put emphasis on the group, others encourage individual achievements. There are many cultural rules operating in your life.

Do you like how your rules allow you to act toward other groups? We are often amused or irritated by the customs of foreigners, from beginning dinner after normal American bedtime in Latin countries to the accepted practice of bribes in many parts of the world. Eating with the correct hand in Muslim countries and where to point the chopsticks in parts of Asia are things that Westerners don't ordinarily think about, thus they are strange and, to Western rules, unnatural and unnecessary. As people travel and learn to accept differences as only different and not inferior, Roots becomes a stable base from which to appreciate differences and make them enlightening rather than divisive, and the wind gives you just the right lift, so you can soar away from prejudice toward knowledge.

RELIGION AND MORALS

This section defines our religious and moral rules. A religious rule:

1. Defines God and/or how we came to exist.
2. Defines what happens after death.
3. Instills a value for human existence.
4. Lists expected behaviors

If you are not religious, list your own set of rules conceptualizing life/death and your moral behavior. If you like, you may include any other aspects you think are important for your spiritual rules. For example, one rule might be: What I do during my life determines what happens to me after I die.

List your two major religious rules.

1.

2.

What do we have so far? You have listed only a few of the rules that define your ethnic and religious background. Let me ask you two questions to put your efforts into a clearer perspective. Have your rules changed much over the years? Do you have the sense that they have kept up with your increased knowledge and awareness? You should be able to see how they have matured since they were first formed when you were a child. For example, your ideas of God, Heaven, and Hell have probably changed since you attended religious school and thought of God as a wise old man and heaven as a place like an amusement park where you could get free ice cream and all the cotton candy you could eat.

WHAT DOES IT ALL MEAN?

If you want to fit into society, you must fulfill the expectations of your roots and the wind. If you want a life that is truly yours, you must become independent of these forces. You may end up not changing much after this process—if you like most of what your roots contain. But if you want to create your own life, you'll take a hard look at the Diabolical Duo.

Another issue is that your personal rules need to evolve over time in a way that considers your growth and changing roles. You may have noticed, for example, how your gender rules changed over time (they did, didn't they?).

Review all the rules you have written so far to see if you still agree with them. Decide if any of your listed rules are really part of your roots and the wind. If so, pencil in some changes. Then put this book down for a while and do things with people and keep one eye on why you're doing these things.

(A little while later)

What kind of rule (ethnic, sex role, etc.) did you operate from most in the last few days?

What do you like about the rule?

PERSONAL WISDOM

You have now taken a good look at the important elements of your roots and the wind. Do you understand how many, how powerful, how tricky these rules are? Do you realize the importance of identifying the rules of your roots and making sure to keep the good and eliminate the bad? You know, of course, that the wind tempts you every day with her evil smile, false eyelashes and gives you a quick push when you're not looking (and even when you are).

Remember these rules exercises every so often. It will be helpful to ask yourself periodically why you did what you just did or thought what you thought. I get irritated when people are not courteous, then remind myself that just because I work hard to be thoughtful doesn't mean everyone else should make it a priority.

So, what is personal wisdom? It is the ability to separate yourself from all the rules, expectations, limitations, prejudices, biases, and on and on that have been meticulously provided by your roots and the wind. Personal wisdom is not selecting "all of the above" in the great test of life but choosing what is right for you. Personal wisdom requires constant vigilance against outside influences, automatic behavior, and useless measurement. It demands accepting the differences, even the failings of others, as well as all the blemishes you see in the mirror.

These few pages have only begun the process. Your roots have given you a world to live in, some of it good, some bad. The wind is always there offering suggestions, some helpful, some harmful. Whenever you find yourself unhappy or resentful, look for one of the Diabolical Duo lurking in the shadows. Get rid of whichever one it is; this is your time.

Review your Personal Truths every few months, when you find yourself doing things that don't work as well as you think they should, or when facing especially difficult decisions.

If you discover a bad truth in your Personal Truths:

1. Erase the old truth
2. Write a new one
3. Evaluate the new truth for a few weeks
4. If it works, great
5. If you don't like the results, write a better version and test that one
6. Repeat this process until you are satisfied

These truths are only a sampling of the thousands of truths that define who you are. They are your road map to living a life you can be proud of. As you travel your road, you'll discover many new things, but like any road, some parts will be bad, and some will be wonderful. Thus, parts of you, you will want to change, parts of you, you will want to keep forever.

Use your personal truths like guideposts and milestones, and all your moments will be the best you can make them. It sounds like a grand way to live.

We'll leave each other after one more quote from our long-dead friend Montaigne:

Lend yourself to others but give yourself to yourself.

About the Author

Bob Brown has been searching for the meaning of life for over fifty years. He found much of it living with his wife Deena and various animals, wild and domestic, north of Seattle.

His undergraduate degree is from the University of Michigan, a doctorate from the United States International University and his pre- and post-doctoral internships were at the University of Michigan Neuropsychiatric Institute.

He was an Honorary Reader at the University of St. Andrews in the early 1990s. He was the co-founder and executive director of the nonprofit Keepers of the Game.

He has written golf books, management books, a few novels, two memoirs and is active teaching and consulting in organizational and leadership development and how to live your best life.

www.ingramcontent.com/pod-product-compliance
Lightning Source LLC
Chambersburg PA
CBHW021045090426
42738CB00006B/198